The E♦Z Legal Guide to

IMMIGRATION

Valerie Hope Goldstein

E♦Z Legal Books

Deerfield Beach, Florida

Distributed by E-Z Legal Forms, Inc.
Manufactured in the United States of America

WHEN YOU NEED IT IN WRITING! is a trademark of E-Z Legal Forms, Inc.

... when you need it in writing! ™

1 2 3 4 5 6 7 8 9 10   **CPC**

Library of Congress Catalog Card Number: 94-061875
The E-Z Legal Guide to Immigration

        p.   cm.

ISBN 1-56382-413-2: $14.95

Title: The E-Z Legal Guide to Immigration.
Author: Valerie Hope Goldstein

Important facts

E-Z Legal products are designed to provide authoritative and accurate information in regard to the subject matter covered. However, neither this nor any other publication can take the place of an attorney on important legal matters.

Information in this guide has been carefully compiled from sources believed to be reliable, but the accuracy of the information is not guaranteed, as laws and regulations may change or be subject to differing interpretations.

Why not have your attorney review this guide? We encourage it.

Limited warranty and disclaimer

This is a self-help legal product and is intended to be used by the consumer for his or her own benefit. Use of this product to benefit a second party may be considered the unauthorized practice of law.

As with any legal matter, common sense should determine whether you need the assistance of an attorney. We urge you to consult with an attorney whenever large amounts of money are involved or on any matter when you do not understand how to properly complete a form or question its adequacy to protect you.

It is understood that by using this legal guide you are acting as your own attorney. Accordingly, the publisher, author, distributor and retailer shall have neither liability nor responsibility to any party for any loss or damage caused or alleged to be caused by use of this guide. This guide is sold with the understanding that the publisher, author, distributor and retailer are not engaged in rendering legal services. If legal services or other expert assistance are required, the services of a competent professional should be sought.

Money-back guarantee

E-Z Legal Forms offers you a limited guarantee. If you consider E-Z Legal Forms to be defective in any way, you may return your purchase to us within 30 days for a full refund of the list or purchase price, whichever is lower. In no event shall our liability – or the liability of any retailer – exceed the purchase price of the product. Use of the product constitutes acceptance of these terms.

Copyright Permission Certificate

The purchaser of this guide is hereby authorized to reproduce in any form or by any means, electronic or mechanical, including photocopying, all forms and documents contained in this guide, provided it is for nonprofit, educational or private use. Such reproduction requires no further permission from the publisher and/or payment of any permission fee.

The reproduction of any form or document in any other publication intended for sale is prohibited without the written permission of the publisher.

Publication for nonprofit use should provide proper attribution to E-Z Legal Forms.

Barry R. Chesler, President, E-Z Legal Forms

Immigration

Table
of contents

How to use this E-Z Legal Guide

E-Z Legal Guides can help you achieve an important legal objective conveniently, efficiently and economically. But it is nevertheless important for you to properly use this guide if you are to avoid later difficulties.

Step-by-step instructions for using this guide:

1 Carefully read all information, warnings and disclaimers concerning the legal forms in this guide. If after thorough examination you decide that you have circumstances that are not covered by the forms in this guide, or you do not feel confident about preparing your own documents, consult an attorney.

2 Before filling out a form, make several copies of the original to practice on, and for future use and updates. You should also make copies of the completed forms. Create a record-keeping system for both sets of copies.

3 Complete each blank on each legal form. Do not skip over inapplicable blanks or lines intended to be completed. If the blank is inapplicable, mark "N/A" or "None" or use a dash. This shows you have not overlooked the item.

4 Always use pen or type on legal documents. Never use pencil.

5 Avoid erasing or crossing out anything you've written on final documents.

6 It is important to remember that on legal contracts or agreements between parties all terms and conditions must be clearly stated. Provisions may not be enforceable unless in writing. All parties to the agreement should receive a copy.

7 You may find more specific instructions within this guide for completing some forms. These instructions are for your benefit and protection, so follow them closely.

8 You will find a helpful glossary of terms at the end of this guide. Refer to this glossary if you encounter unfamiliar terms.

9 Always keep legal documents in a safe place and in a location known to your spouse, family, executor or attorney.

Introduction

Of the millions of foreign residents who are issued visas each year, many decide that they would like to live and work in the United States permanently. Most of those who are successful have immediate family members who are U.S. citizens, or have special training in a profession sought by U.S. employees.

The United States government grants permanent residence to an immigrant in two steps: first, by issuing a green card and, later, by granting citizenship.

This guide discusses the rules and application procedures to obtain your green card and to be granted U.S. citizenship. It can be a complicated, frustrating and time-consuming process, but this guide shows you how the system works.

You may find that you are unfamiliar with some of the words and phrases used in this guide. Immigration law has its own special language. For this reason we have provided a complete glossary at the back of this guide. Wherever possible, this guide uses the words and phrases on the government immigration forms. If you take the time to understand the information in this guide, you will find that selecting a green card category and filling out the correct forms is easy.

In order to enter the United States legally, whether you are visiting for a few days or immigrating for a lifetime, you must obtain an entry visa. Entry visas are issued only by United States consulates and embassies in foreign countries. Citizens of certain countries, such as Mexico and Canada, are allowed to enter for short stays without visas. This guide assumes that you have already been issued an entry visa and that you are in the United States legally.

Once you are in the United States, you may begin the process of applying for permanent residence for yourself, your spouse, your children, and other relatives who may still be living in a foreign country. This guide will be of great help to anyone trying to understand the U.S. Immigration category system and the application process.

Do you need a lawyer?

Many aliens applying for green cards wonder if they need to hire a lawyer. The answer depends upon the complexity of your situation. If you have been denied residence in the past, have been previously deported, or are subject to the Excludability Rule, then it makes good sense to get the opinion of a legal expert. A knowledgeable attorney may be able to find an exception to the Excludability Rule that would allow you to live in the United States. If you intend to apply for a green card as an investor, an attorney may help you decide if you are eligible and if your investment is a sound one.

Many of the simpler green card categories are easy enough to understand without hiring an attorney. You may apply for these on your own. It is especially easy to apply for green cards for immediate family members of U.S. citizens.

The documents that you will be required to submit must be in English. While copies are acceptable, you must show the originals if requested to do so.

For those who want to remain in the United States, there are many opportunities to obtain a green card. Read through this guide, decide where you fit into the immigration picture, apply accordingly, and reap the same benefits and privileges as those born in America.

The category system

The first step in the process of establishing permanent residency in the United States is to apply for your green card. Officially known as an "Alien Registration Receipt Card," it is called the "green card" because it used to be green, although it no longer is. No matter its color, it is a registration card issued by the U.S. government permitting an alien to live and work permanently in the United States. However, a green card does not mean that the alien is a citizen. The holder cannot vote, for example. The green card may be canceled if the alien remains outside of the United States too long or commits a crime.

The Immigration Act of 1990 has changed the green card procedure in several important ways. It seeks to reunite families separated by the immigration process. Illegal aliens granted legal amnesty through special acts in the 1980s may, in some cases, bring their spouses and minor children to the United States. Illegitimate children of aliens are also considered eligible for immigration under the new law.

Immigration officials have also sharply changed their views on labor. The focus is now in favor of more skilled workers. Those with advanced technical and professional training are especially in demand. The number of green cards issued to unskilled laborers continues to decline.

The Immigration Act has tried to evenly represent the racial and ethnic makeup of aliens in America. Although many aliens today still arrive from Europe, many more come from Latin America, Africa, and Asia. One of the tools immigration officials use to accomplish this equality is called the Diversity Lottery. This lottery selects names of aliens at random, giving them a chance to become United States citizens through nothing more than sheer luck. Even those with no relatives in the United States or with no professional training have a chance at the American dream through this lottery.

The two government agencies that are responsible for issuing green cards to aliens are the Immigration and Naturalization Service (INS) and the Department of Labor (DOL).

Immigration and Naturalization Service

The INS, part of the Department of Justice, handles applications for green cards. The INS helps those with visas file for a change in status. Paperwork is processed at local offices, then passed on to larger district offices. Applications that do not require interviews are handled at special regional service centers. Aliens usually mail their applications to one of the local offices. (While it is possible to contact INS offices by phone, the phone lines are busy and the wait can be very long.)

The Department of Labor

If you are coming to the United States to work, your U.S. employer must apply for labor certification or attestation through the DOL. The DOL seeks to uphold the rights of American workers in immigration-related matters. Your employer's request will only be approved if it appears absolutely necessary for a foreigner to take the job. The certification process normally takes a few months to complete. If turned down, your employer may file an appeal with the DOL or wait several more months and file another certification.

Visa categories

The entire U.S. immigration system is based upon a strict class of visa categories. Each category has specific requirements. The most basic principle of this system is that in order to be eligible for a green card, and eventually for citizenship, you must prove that you fit into one of the categories. There are no exceptions.

The key to finding a category to fit into is to know the requirements. Even if you don't qualify now, by knowing what is required you may be able to change your circumstances so that you will eventually qualify. There are eight major green card categories presently available for those who wish permanent residency:

1) Green cards for family members

2) Marital green cards

3) Adoption green cards

4) Employment green cards

5) Investor green cards

6) Diversity (lottery) green cards

7) Sanctuary green cards

8) Special green cards

General filing procedures

There are often more applicants than available green cards. Quotas limit how many green cards may be given to any one group of people. Quotas determine who gets to immigrate first. If your green card category has a quota, you must take the first step in the filing procedure (usually filing a petition) and then wait for a slot to become available. Some applicants wait for several months; others may have to wait ten years or longer. You cannot speed up the waiting process under a quota. Shortcuts are sometimes possible in completing and filing paperwork, but quotas must simply be waited out.

Whether your wait is ten weeks or ten years, you must remain a legal alien at all times, never violating your temporary visa status, and always having a valid I-94 card. An I-94 card is evidence that an alien has entered the U.S. legally and also indicates how long he or she may stay in the United States. Once you have been given the right to live permanently in the United States, you are considered an alien.

The two-step process

The filing process for obtaining a green card consists of two steps. Step one begins with the petition. When you file a petition with the INS, you are asking for permission to go to step two, which is the filing of the formal application. You cannot file an application for a green card unless your petition is approved. Step one ends when your petition is either accepted or rejected. If it is accepted, you will be given a priority date. Step two begins when you receive that priority date, since it is the date to submit your final application to the INS. Do not submit your application before this date.

Your priority date

Your priority date will be based upon two factors: your category and your country.

1) **Your category.** Immediate family members of U.S. citizens have no quotas and no waits. More distant relatives, on the other hand, must usually wait at least several years for their priority dates to come up. In a similar way, highly skilled professional workers have shorter waits for employment-based green cards than unskilled laborers.

2) **Your native country.** Filipinos and Mexicans often face longer waits than other nationalities. Because their countries send many applicants to the U.S. each year, there are more citizens of these countries who want green cards than there are green cards available.

Some categories require an interview as part of the filing process. If an interview is required, the INS will notify you of the place and time it is to be held. Once officials are satisfied that you have met all green card requirements, your passport will be stamped to show you are a permanent resident. You will receive your green card by mail in a few months.

Green card holders may, in turn, sponsor relatives for green cards. They may not vote in elections or hold government office, however. Once you have had a green card for five years you may apply for U.S. citizenship (in some cases you do not have to wait this long. See Chapter 12, "Becoming a U.S. Citizen," for more information.)

Highlight

Immediate family members of U.S. citizens have no quotas and no waits. More distant relatives, on the other hand, must usually wait at least several years for their priority dates to come up.

Green cards for family members

Foreigners with relatives who are either U.S. citizens or green card holders are eligible to receive family green cards. Family green cards are divided into three classes: cards for Immediate Relatives, cards for Preference Relatives, and cards for Accompanying Relatives.

1) The first family member category, Immediate Relatives, has the highest priority. Immediate Relatives include:

A. Spouses (husbands or wives) of U.S. citizens

B. Chidren of U.S. citizens, unmarried and under the age of 21, both natural and adopted (if the adoption took place at least two years before filing and the child was under 16 at the time)

C. Parents of U.S. citizens over the age of 21

D. Some widows and widowers of U.S. citizens. (A widow or widower who was married to a U.S. citizen for at least two years, has not remarried, and applied for a green card on or before November 29, 1992, may in some cases still be eligible. Check with an attorney.)

E. Stepparents and stepchildren of U.S. citizens (if the marriage took place before the child's 18th birthday).

Immediate Relatives do not normally face quotas. They usually have short or no waiting period before they receive their green cards. Please note that the spouses and children of Immediate Relatives do not automatically receive green cards. Each must apply and qualify separately. Spouses are usually issued two-year conditional green cards that may be converted into permanent green cards after the trial period is over.

2) The second family member category, Preference Relatives, has the next highest priority. Preference Relatives include:

A. Family First Preference: Unmarried adult children of U.S. citizens. This category has a quota of 23,400 visas each year. Because few people fall under Family First Preference, the wait for a green card is usually a short one. However, if you are from Mexico or the Philippines, the wait is at least five years.

B. Family Second Preference (2-A): Spouses and unmarried minor children of green card holders

C. Family Second Preference (2-B): Unmarried adult children of green card holders. Priority is given to the 2-A category (88,000 out of 114,000 Second Preference green cards, or 71 percent, go to spouses and minor children). There is normally a 2-to-3-year waiting period. Mexicans and Filipinos applying for 2-A or 2-B Family green cards do not face a longer wait than other nationalities.

D. Family Third Preference: Married children (any age) of U.S. citizens. There are only 23,400 green cards available each year in this category. There are many more applicants than green cards. Because of this the wait is at least two years. Filipinos and Mexicans must usually wait at least eight years.

E. Family Fourth Preference: Brothers or sisters of adult U.S. citizens. There are 65,000 green cards available each year to brothers and sisters of U.S. citizens. As with most categories, there are many more people applying than there are green cards. The wait is often at least ten years, and even longer for Filipinos and Mexicans. When possible, it is recommended that applicants in this category try to find a quicker green card category (e.g. employment) and apply for that instead.

3) The third family member category, Accompanying Relatives, has the lowest priority. Accompanying Relatives include:

A. Spouses of Preference Relatives

B. Unmarried minor children of Preference Relatives

Although spouses and children of immediate family members must qualify separately for green cards, spouses and children of Preference Relatives receive them automatically. You must show a birth or marriage certificate as proof of the relationship when you apply.

A special note on Amnesty Relatives

On May 4, 1988, any alien who was in the U.S. illegally received a general pardon, or "amnesty," and became eligible for a green card. If you are in

Highlight

Because few people fall under Family First Preference, the wait for a green card is usually a short one.

this classification, contact your local INS office for the latest information.

Exploring other options

Many families are torn apart because some members are eligible to immigrate to the U.S. and others are not. This is a sad but true part of the immigration picture. Keep in mind that family members who do not qualify for family-related green cards may be eligible through employment, marriage, diversity lottery, or several of the other green card categories available. If your family is facing this separation dilemma, consult with a knowledgeable attorney who can look into your available options.

Fathers of illegitimate children have previously faced discrimination by the INS when attempting to prove paternity. However, recent court rulings have now made it easier for unwed fathers involved in the immigration process. You should consult with an attorney if you are in this situation.

Filing for family member green cards

The filing procedure consists of two parts, the petition and the application.

1) **The petition:** The INS calls the person sponsoring you (your U.S. relative) a "petitioner" because he or she is working with you in the immigration process and may file the necessary forms on your behalf. Your U.S. relative should file a visa petition on your behalf at the nearest INS office. Use form I-130. Include birth and/or marital certificates showing your relationship (and the relationship of any relative immigrating with you) to the U.S. petitioner. A separate petition must be filed for immigrating stepchildren.

2) **The application:** Once your priority date comes up and your petition is approved, submit the following documents to the INS:

- Form I-485
- Form G-325A
- Form I-765 (if you wish to work)
- Proof that your petition was approved by the INS
- Documents originally filed as part of your petition (except proof of U.S. relative's citizenship)
- Three photographs of yourself and each accompanying relative
- Form I-34 showing financial support, proof of a U.S. job offer, or bank statements showing your ability to support yourself without working

• I-94 cards for yourself and each accompanying relative

You and each accompanying relative between the ages of 14 and 79 will be fingerprinted at the INS offices as proof of identity.

Once you submit your application for a green card you must remain wherever you are until the application process is complete. If you are already in the United States and leave the country after you apply, the INS will consider your green card application to be withdrawn and you will have to start the process over again.

If you must leave the country during this process, submit Form I-512 to your nearest INS office, along with three photos of yourself and proof of the emergency requiring you to leave the United States. If the INS approves, you will be given "advance parole," allowing you to leave the U.S. temporarily without affecting your green card application.

The long wait involved for some green cards for family members often makes it worthwhile to investigate other green card categories. If you think you may be eligible for an employment, investor, or special immigrant green card, consider applying for one of these instead.

Highlight

The long wait involved for some green cards for family members often makes it worthwhile to investigate other green card categories.

Marital green cards

Spouses of U.S. citizens may apply for green cards before or at the time of their marriage. K visas benefit those couples who are unable to get married in the foreign fiance's native country, but who will marry in the U.S. within 90 days of arrival. Most couples, however, apply directly for a green card.

Unlike green cards issued to other family members, marital green cards are usually issued conditionally. Upon marrying a U.S. citizen, a foreigner becomes eligible for a conditional two-year green card. This means that there is a two-year waiting period, or trial period, before the INS will issue a permanent green card. The spouse who is a U.S. citizen must petition the nearest INS office on the foreign spouse's behalf. Once the foreign spouse receives conditional approval, he or she may work and live legally in the United States until the two years are up. He or she has a green card but is not considered to be a permanent resident until the two-year trial period is over.

Filing for a marital green card

The filing procedure consists of two parts, the petition and the application.

1) **The petition:** The following forms should be filed with the nearest INS office at the time of the marriage:

- Form I-130
- Form G-325A
- Proof of spouse's U.S. citizenship or green card

- The foreign spouse's birth certificate
- The U.S. spouse's birth certificate
- Copies of marriage and any previous divorce certificates
- One recent photograph of each spouse

2) **The application:** The foreign spouse should apply for entry into the United States. (See Chapter 2, "Green Cards For Family Members," for details of the application process.)

Removing your conditional status 

Within 90 days of the two-year card's expiration, the foreign spouse should file the following documents with the INS:

Form I-751 (to remove conditional status; this must be signed by both spouses)

Proof that the marriage is still valid (e.g. joint bank account statements, proof of joint home ownership, or tax returns)

The appropriate filing fee

The application interview

As part of the application process for a marital green card, you may have to be interviewed by the INS. You will receive a letter stating the date and time of your interview. It is important that both spouses appear at the application interview. You and your spouse may be interviewed separately, but your answers must agree. Interviews are very detailed and the interviewers tend to ask questions about some personal areas of your married life. Questions may include:

- How did the two of you first meet?
- What sort of activities do you enjoy?
- Do you have the same friends?
- What does your home look like?

Interviewers may also ask about your intimate relationship with your spouse, but they are not supposed to go beyond the boundaries of good taste. Nevertheless, refusing to answer an interviewer's questions could cause your application to be turned down.

Highlight

It is important that both spouses appear at the application interview. You and your spouse may be interviewed separately, but your answers must agree.

CHAPTER 3

The interview should last about half an hour. When the interview is finished, the INS will make its final decision regarding your green card status. If the decision is favorable, your two-year condition will be removed and you will become a permanent U.S. resident.

Fraudulent marriages

Marital green card applicants will be watched closely during the two years between the petition and the application. The INS estimates that at least half of all immigrant marriages occur solely for the purpose of obtaining a green card. This type of marriage is illegal. The INS is quick to deport foreign spouses whose marriages are obvious frauds set up for immigration purposes only. Those who take part in such marriages may also face criminal prosecution.

If you are not still married when the two years are up and it is time to apply for permanent residency, you will have to prove one of the following to remain in the U.S.:

- That although you are now divorced, you entered into the marriage in good faith. (In other words, you did not get married just to get a green card.)
- That deportation will cause you greater hardship than it would to most other deportees
- That you were abused by your U.S. spouse

Foreign spouses who divorce once the two-year condition is removed from their green card are not usually subject to deportation. For this reason it is advisable to delay a pending divorce until the two-year condition is removed.

Persons who get married during deportation proceedings may remain in the U.S., but they will face the strictest possible examination from the INS. They will have to prove beyond a doubt that the purpose of their marriage was not to stop the deportation process.

If your sponsor dies

If you are the spouse of a U.S. citizen who dies during your green card process, you may continue your application process if you were married for at least two years. If you are the spouse of a green card holder who dies during your application process, you are not usually eligible to continue your application process. Check with an attorney if your sponsoring spouse dies during the application process.

Adoption green cards

There are special rules that parents must follow when filing on behalf of adopted foreign children. The INS has divided all adopted children into two classes: orphans and non-orphans.

Adopted orphans

Adopted orphans are defined by the INS this way: Both of the child's natural parents are dead, or the child has been legally abandoned, or the parents have put the child up for adoption.

Green card requirements for orphans include:

- The child must be living outside of the U.S. at the time of adoption.
- The child must be under 16 years old at the time of the adoption.
- One of the adopting parents has to be a U.S. citizen. If the adopting parent is single, he or she must be at least 25 years old.

Before you meet your child

Many couples intend to adopt a child from a specific foreign country but have not met the child at the time they file their petition. This is perfectly acceptable under U.S. law. It is suggested that you file a "preliminary petition" (including form I-600A) before you go to the foreign country to select your child. Bring all of the required documents with you on your trip so you may file an application at the child's home consulate.

In the United States, state adoption laws vary. Follow your state's pre-adoption laws. Sometimes you have to be interviewed or have an official from the adoption agency visit your home. Arrange this before you apply.

Filing for an orphan's green card

The filing procedure consists of two parts: the petition and the application.

1) **The petition:** Submit the following to the INS or the child's home consulate:

- Form I-600
- Form I-600A (advance processing)
- The child's birth certificate
- The birth certificate of one of the adoptive parents (or proof of U.S. residency)
- The adoptive parents' marriage certificate
- Proof of a home visit by an approved private adoption agency
- Proof that all pre-adoption requirements have been met
- Proof that the child may be adopted legally (this may include proof that the natural parents are dead, legal papers ending their rights as parents, or proof that the child was abandoned)

The INS will also fingerprint adoptive parents as proof of identity.

2) **The application:** Once your petition is approved and you have met your child in his or her home country, file the following at the nearest U.S. consulate:

- Form OF-179 or OF-230-I
- Form OF-230
- Form I-134
- Proof that your petition was approved
- All documents that you originally submitted as part of the petition process
- A valid passport for the orphan
- Three photographs of the orphan

Adopted non-orphans

Adopted non-orphans are defined by the INS this way: A child under 16 who has already been adopted by a U.S. citizen or green card holder. The child must have lived with the adoptive parents for at least two years before the application is filed. Unlike the orphan category, non-orphans have already been legally adopted. The petitioning parent does not have to be a

Highlight

Unlike the orphan category, non-orphans have already been legally adopted. The petitioning parent does not have to be a U.S. citizen as long as he or she holds a permanent green card.

CHAPTER 4

U.S. citizen as long as he or she holds a permanent green card. There is no minimum age requirement for single adoptive parents in this category.

The investigation

The adoptive parents of a non-orphan must be investigated by a U.S.-licensed private adoption agency as part of the procedure. If this has already been done as part of the adoption process, the requirement may be waived. However, if the adoption took place in a foreign country or the adoptive parents live in a state where such investigations are not required as part of the adoption process, an investigation will have to be done before the child may receive a green card.

Age

Although the non-orphan must have been under age 16 at the time of the adoption, the child may be over 16 at the time the adoptive parent(s) petition for a green card. The petition and application process is the same as for all family green cards, except that in the case of adoption, the two-year minimum, the investigation, and the age requirements must also be met.

Special note: Any adoption process may sometimes become complicated, especially if you are adopting from a Third World country or from a country torn by political unrest. In these cases you should consult with an attorney specializing in foreign adoptions.

Highlight

Any adoption process may sometimes become complicated, especially if you are adopting from a Third World country or from a country torn by political unrest.

Employment green cards

Before you apply for a green card in most employment-based categories, your employer has to show the Department of Labor (DOL) that it was impossible to find American workers to fill the position. Proving this is known as the Labor Certification Process. It requires placing three types of advertisements seeking to hire American workers.

Your employer should submit Form ETA-750 to the local Department of Employment and Training (DET) providing a complete description of the job. The DET will then assign a number for the job and send a letter with complete instructions on how your employer should place the advertisements. Your employer then has 45 days to place the ads.

1) Local job service ads: The DET will list the job on its statewide computerized job bank. Anyone who submits a resume within 30 days of the advertisement and seems qualified will be referred to the employer for an interview. The employer must either hire that person or explain to the DET in writing why that person was not hired.

2) Classified ads: Your employer must place an ad in the classified section of the local newspaper for three days in a row. The ad should list the qualifications, duties, hours, and salary for the job. Instead of publishing the employer's name and address, the ad should list the reference number assigned by the DET, and have all applicants send their resumes directly to this number. Anyone the DET decides is qualified will be referred to the employer for an interview. The employer must again explain in writing why an applicant does not qualify if he or she is not hired.

3) Company employee ads: The final ad is to be posted in a noticeable spot, such as on an employee bulletin board, at the employer's place of business. It should be the same as the ad that appears in the newspaper, except that instead of listing the DET it should give the name of a person at the company to whom interested employees may apply. This ad must remain posted for at least ten working days. If a labor union is involved with the company, it must also receive a copy of the ad. The employer must again interview all qualified American applicants.

Precertified jobs

Each year the DET chooses up to ten occupations for which work shortages exist and for which green cards are precertified. That means that these jobs do not require Labor Certification. Check with the DOL for an updated list of these occupations.

Qualifying for an employment green card

There is a quota of 140,000 for employment-based green cards. These are mostly available to skilled workers with a permanent job offer from a U.S. employer. Applicants must have the appropriate background and training, including any necessary degrees or licenses. Most—but not all— jobs offered through green cards require at least a bachelor's degree and several years of work experience in that field. If you do not have a college degree, a fairly long work history, or experience in a profession that requires an advanced education, your chance of getting a green card through employment may be difficult.

Your U.S. employer may be a corporation, an organization, or an individual. Generally, you may not hire yourself as a worker unless you are the owner of a large business employing several American workers (also see Chapter 6, "Investor Green Cards"). Individuals hired by relatives face strict examination from the INS.

Your employer must pay you a salary that is within 5 percent of what American workers in your occupation normally earn. Your employer must be able to pay this salary without hurting the financial health of the business. It is also important that your employer be willing to share tax documents with immigration officials and agree to participate in the lengthy and sometimes complicated Labor Certification process. Finally, your employer must realize that due to quota and certification requirements, it will take at least one year for your green card to be approved; only then will you be able to start working.

Employment green cards are divided into three main categories:

Highlight

If you do not have a college degree, a fairly long work history, or experience in a profession that requires an advanced education, your chance of getting a green card through employment may be difficult.

1) First Preference, consisting of employees who have extraordinary ability, outstanding professors and researchers, and multinational executives and managers.

2) Second Preference, consisting of employees who are professionals with advanced degrees and persons of exceptional ability.

3) Third Preference, consisting of professional workers without advanced degrees, skilled workers, and unskilled workers.

The first employment category, First Preference employees (priority workers), has the highest priority. There are 40,000 green cards in this category, which include:

A. Persons of extraordinary ability, including famous scientists, artists, business people, teachers, and athletes. You must be an internationally recognized performer or expert in your field. Nobel Prize and Academy Award winners, famous athletes and founders of large, highly successful businesses qualify. People in this category do not need to have a job waiting in the U.S. to apply. No Labor Certification process is required, and the wait for a green card is short.

B. Outstanding university professors or researchers, including professors and academic, industrial, or scientific researchers. You must be a professor or researcher associated with a well known institution employing at least two other researchers. No Labor Certification process is required.

C. Multinational executives or managers, including executives and managers who have been employed for at least three years. Managers must do all of the following:

1) Supervise an organization or department

2) Oversee other supervisors or important company functions

3) Have the authority to hire or fire

4) Be involved in daily, senior level decision-making

Executives must do all of the following:

1) Direct or supervise managers

2) Set organizational policies

3) Have major decision-making authority

4) Be directly responsible to the stockholders or a board of trustees

To further qualify, you must take a position as a manager or executive with a U.S. branch, subsidiary, or affiliate in a foreign country, and your

---

Highlight

Nobel Prize and Academy Award winners, famous athletes and founders of large, highly successful businesses qualify. People in this category do not need to have a job waiting in the U.S. to apply.

U.S. employer must have been in business for at least one year. No Labor Certification is required.

The second employment category, Second Preference employees, has the next highest priority. You must have a definite job offer from a U.S. employer to be eligible. There are 40,000 green cards in this category, which include:

A. Advanced-degree professionals in areas such as law and medicine. Labor certification is usually required. Engineers and nurses do not qualify unless they have received a postgraduate degree from an accredited institution.

B. Persons of exceptional ability, including distinguished scientists, artists and businesspersons. Those not famous enough to qualify for green cards under the First Preference Extraordinary Ability category may qualify under this category. In your home country you must be recognized as a leader in your field, but you need not have achieved international fame. If you are able to prove that you will make an important contribution to culture, business, or education in the United States, your employer need not go through the Labor Certification process.

The third employment category, Third Preference employees, has the lowest priority. There are 40,000 green cards in this category, which include:

A. Professional workers without advanced degrees, including architects, lawyers, medical technicians or therapists, computer systems analysts, accountants, chemists, fashion designers, hotel managers and pilots of large aircraft. Those included in this group must have a bachelor's degree but can have less than five years work experience. You must already have been offered a job when you apply for the green card. If your degree came from a foreign school, you will need to get an independent academic evaluation. (See the back of this guide for the names and addresses of acceptable evaluators). Labor Certification is usually required.

B. Skilled workers, including people who do not have a degree but who work in occupations requiring at least two years of specialized training. Jobs with two-year apprenticeships may qualify. Check with your local DET for a list of approved jobs in this category. Labor Certification is usually required.

C. Unskilled workers. You do not need specialized training to qualify for this group, but you must show that you have the skills necessary to do the required work. Some jobs may require some vocational training. If they

Highlight

Engineers and nurses do not qualify unless they have received a postgraduate degree from an accredited institution.

do, you must complete such training before applying for a green card. Labor Certification is required.

Where to find a job

The DOL publishes updated lists of Schedule A and Schedule B jobs in which there is a shortage of skilled and unskilled workers. Check with the INS or the DOL for a current list.

Schedule A lists jobs for skilled workers. The two most common jobs that appear on this list are for medical therapists and nurses. Jobs from the Schedule-A list do not need Labor Certification.

Schedule-B jobs do not require skilled workers but do require Labor Certification. Cooks, kitchen workers, auto attendants, assemblers, bartenders, maids, chauffeurs, and receptionists are only a few of the jobs on this list. As with Schedule-A jobs, the list is constantly changing.

Filing for an employment green card

Your employer must file two forms for you to get an employment green card: the petition and the application.

1) **The petition:** Once your U.S. employer receives Labor Certification approval, he or she should submit a petition to the INS on your behalf, consisting of the following documents:

- Form I-140
- Proof of Labor Certification approval, or proof that the job qualifies under Schedule A, Schedule B, or the Recertification Program
- All documents submitted as part of Labor Certification process
- Your educational transcript(s)
- Proof that you have a professional license or training certificate
- Proof of work experience in your present career
- The employer's latest financial documents (e.g. tax returns, balance sheets)
- First Preference employees with extraordinary ability should submit articles about their achievements and awards
- Professors should submit proof of their tenure at a U.S. university

●Multinational executives should submit proof of a contract with a U.S. employer. (If in the U.S. on an L-1 temporary visa, resubmit everything you filed as part of the visa process.)

●Schedule A workers should submit proof of a license (if applicable) or proof that they qualify for a license. Nurses must show proof of a U.S. or Canadian degree from an accredited school of nursing, or that they have passed the Commission on Graduates of Foreign Nursing Schools (CGFNS) equivalency exam.

2) **The application:** Once your employer has submitted your petition, you must wait for your priority date to come up before applying to the INS for a green card. When it is time for you to apply, submit the following documents to the INS:

●Form I-485

●Form I-325A

●Proof that your petition was approved

●Results of a medical exam for yourself and each accompanying relative

●Birth certificates for yourself and each accompanying relative

●A valid passport for yourself and each accompanying relative

●A letter from your U.S. employer verifying that the job is still open

●Three photos of yourself, and of each accompanying relative

●I-94 cards for yourself and for each accompanying relative

●A filing fee (check with INS for correct amount)

In addition, you and each accompanying relative between the ages of 14 and 79 will be fingerprinted by the INS. This serves as proof of identity.

Investor green cards

E ach year there are 10,000 two-year conditional green cards available to foreigners who are willing to invest large amounts of money in new American businesses. To be eligible for a green card, this type of investment must meet the four following requirements:

1) **Minimum investment.** The minimum required investment is $500,000 in cash, bank notes, CDs or merchandise. As an investor, you may borrow the money if you agree to remain personally liable and if the loan is not based upon the assets of the business in which you are investing. Several investors may jointly invest in the same business, but each will still have to invest a minimum amount of $500,000.

The location of the business is an important factor. Investment requirements are lowest in rural areas and highest in urban areas. Depending upon the rate of unemployment in the location you choose, your minimum investment may be as high as $3 million.

2) **Ten American workers.** The business you start or select must employ at least ten full-time American workers. These ten workers may not include you or your family.

3) **Funds already invested.** Most of your funds should already have been invested by the time you apply for a green card. The business you select should be brand new. If you select an existing business, you must have increased its net worth by at least 40 percent. You may show this increase by raising profits 40 percent or by hiring 40 percent more workers. If the business is troubled and had lost 20 percent of its net worth over the last two years, the 40 percent increase rule will be waived. However, you will still have to invest at least $500,000 and hire ten full-time American workers, regardless of the firm's financial condition.

4) **Legitimate purposes only.** If the INS finds out during the next two years that your business is fraudulent and was only established for green card purposes, your conditional green card will be revoked and you may face immediate deportation. Otherwise, you must apply for removal of the condition 90 days before your conditional green card expires. If you can prove at that time that you still own the business and employ ten American workers, the INS will issue you a permanent green card.

It is important to consult a knowledgeable immigration or corporate attorney before you invest money in an American business. Some investments that appear to be sound may not be, or they may not qualify you for a green card in this category.

Filing for investor green cards 

The filing procedure consists of two parts, the petition and the application.

1) **The petition:** Submit the following documents to the INS Regional Service Center nearest your place of business:

- Form I-526
- The current filing fee
- A description of the business you have invested in and a detailed business plan for the next three years
- The Articles of Incorporation, business license, or legal charter for the business in which you have invested
- A notarized affidavit from the official business recordkeeper showing the name of each owner and his or her percentage of ownership in the company
- The lease agreement for the business premises
- Any literature promoting or describing the business
- Bank statements showing the average account balance of the business
- Proof of bank deposits made by the business
- Proof of the source of the deposited funds
- Proof of inventory purchases
- If the business is in a rural or high unemployment area, you need a letter of confirmation from the government
- If the business is a corporation, it must provide copies of all outstanding stock certificates

2) **The application:** Once your petition is approved you may apply for a conditional two-year green card. Submit the following documents to the INS:

- Forms I-485 and G-325A
- Form 765 (if you require advanced work authorization)
- Form I-134 for each accompanying relative
- Proof that your petition was approved
- I-94 cards for you and each accompanying relative
- Birth certificates for the applicant and each accompanying relative. Include birth certificates for your children, even if they are not immigrating with you
- Copies of marriage and any previous divorce certificates
- Medical exam reports for yourself and for each accompanying relative
- A valid passport and three photos of yourself and of each accompanying relative

In addition, the INS will fingerprint you and each accompanying relative between the ages of 14 and 79 as proof of identity.

You must file with the INS to remove the two-year condition within 90 days of the conditional green card's expiration date. Submit Form I-752 with the current filing fee plus proof that you still own your business and are employing at least ten full-time American workers. Once you, the investor, receive a green card, your spouse and children will receive green cards automatically.

Diversity (lottery) green cards

The Immigration Act of 1990 makes green cards available to aliens who don't qualify for permanent residence under any of the other categories. As of January 1, 1995, there are 55,000 lottery green cards available each year. The Department of State uses a computer to randomly select the winners. There is a drawing every year on a date also selected at random. If you receive a green card under this system, your spouse and children receive green cards automatically.

Who is eligible for the lottery? 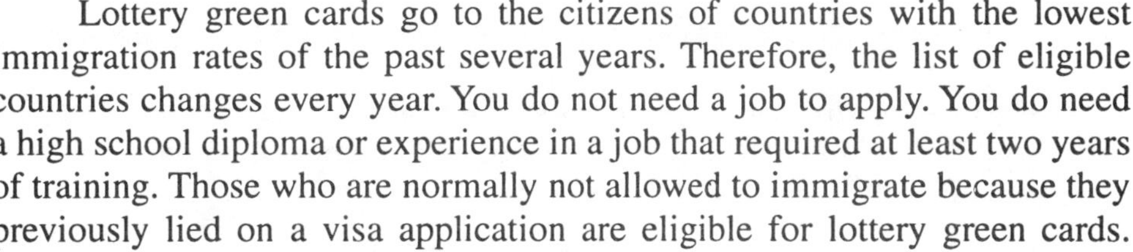

Lottery green cards go to the citizens of countries with the lowest immigration rates of the past several years. Therefore, the list of eligible countries changes every year. You do not need a job to apply. You do need a high school diploma or experience in a job that required at least two years of training. Those who are normally not allowed to immigrate because they previously lied on a visa application are eligible for lottery green cards. (Other excludable people are not eligible.)

Each year the Department of State announces the countries that are eligible for the lottery in the Federal Register and in the news media. The announcements contain the specific dates when you must apply for the lottery and a post office box that serves as the mailing address for your registration.

How to register for the lottery 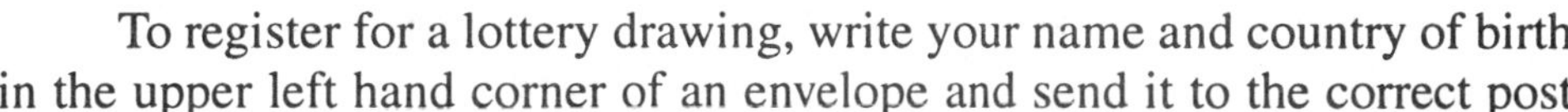

To register for a lottery drawing, write your name and country of birth in the upper left hand corner of an envelope and send it to the correct post office box number. No official form is needed. Put a piece of paper in the envelope listing your:

Full legal name
Date of birth
Place of birth
Mailing address

Include the names, dates, and places of birth of each accompanying relative. Mail the envelope to the Department of State at the address of the special post office box.

Send only one registration per lottery. If you are caught sending more than one, you will be disqualified. Registrations are only good for one lottery. If you are not selected, your registration will not be carried over to the next lottery the following year. If you wish at that time to re-apply, you must send in a new registration.

What are your chances?

The Department of State runs the lottery on a random basis. This means that it doesn't matter whether you are among the first or the last people to register; if your registration is received before the deadline, you have the same chance to be picked as everyone else.

Filing for the lottery green card

If your registration is selected, you must apply for a green card by the following September 30. Submit the following documents to the INS office when you find out you have been selected:

- Forms I-485, I-765, G-325A and OF 230-I
- I-94 cards for yourself and each accompanying relative
- Birth certificates for yourself and for each accompanying relative
- Copies of marriage and any previous divorce certificates
- A valid passport and three recent photos of yourself and each accompanying relative
- A medical exam report for yourself and for each accompanying relative
- Proof of your work experience
- Proof that you have a high school diploma

8

Sanctuary green cards

The four categories of green cards issued to those who face persecution or the threat of persecution in their home countries are: cards for refugees, cards for asylees (those seeking political asylum), cards for parolees, and cards for those with Temporary Protected Status (TPS). Green cards are automatically given to spouses and children of refugees and asylees.

Who qualifies?

Grounds for persecution may include race, religion, political views, nationality, and membership in a social group.

Economic hardship alone will not qualify you for one of these green cards. You must prove either that you are presently being persecuted or that you will be persecuted in the near future. If members of a group you belong to face severe harassment in your home country, you do not have to be singled out. This is proof enough.

Refugees

Refugees fleeing their home country because of persecution are subject to the green card quotas that the U.S. places on foreign countries. These quotas change every year. Many refugees fully deserving of immigration must therefore wait until a new quota is established.

Refugees must apply for their status before coming to the United States. They must show proof of persecution and that they have a sponsor in the United States who is willing to pay for their transportation to the United States. The sponsor must also be willing to support them financially once they arrive. Refugees must also show that they have not resettled permanently in another country during the quota waiting period. If they are permitted to enter the United States, they may apply for a green card one year after arriving in the United States.

Refugees will be contacted by the INS one year after they settle in the United States. At that time they will be interviewed and fingerprinted. If all is in order, they will receive green cards for permanent residence.

Filing for refugee green cards:

Although there is no formal petition process for this category, refugees should submit the following documents to the nearest U.S. consulate or embassy in their home country:

- Form I-590
- Personal identification
- A personal notarized affidavit explaining why you want refugee status
- Affidavits from experts on conditions in your home country (e.g. reports from human rights organizations such as Amnesty International)
- Proof that you have financial sponsorship in the U.S.
- Birth certificates for yourself and for each accompanying relative
- Copies of marriage and any previous divorce certificates for yourself and your spouse.
- Three recent photos of yourself and each accompanying relative

Parolees

Occasionally, those who qualify as refugees face long quotas. If they are in danger in their home country, they may come to the United States as parolees. This is a temporary status and does not lead to a green card. It is simply a safety valve to be used when the quotas are full. Parolees may apply for asylee status once in the United States, but they do not always receive it.

Asylees

Asylees are refugees who are already in the United States as a result of persecution in their home country because of their political beliefs. To be eligible for a green card, asylees must show that they have not resettled permanently in another country. Because asylees must apply for their status after they have arrived in the U.S, they do not have to prove financial sponsorship and they have no quotas to enter the United States. However, they will be placed on a waiting list for a green card and must re-register with the INS for asylee status annually. If at any time during the wait for a green card the INS believes conditions have improved in their home country, asylees may be forced to return home without receiving a green card.

Filing for asylee green cards:

If you are seeking political asylum in the United States, you should submit the following to one of several special INS offices located in California, Florida, Illinois, New Jersey, Texas, or Virginia:

- Form I-589
- Form I-765 (if you want work permission)
- Form G-325 for yourself and each accompanying relative
- Personal identification for yourself and each accompanying relative
- A notarized affidavit explaining why you are seeking political asylum
- Written reports on current persecution in your home country (e.g. reports from human rights organizations such as Amnesty International)
- Newspaper articles on current persecution in your home country
- Birth certificates for yourself and each accompanying relative
- Copies of marriage and any previous divorce certificates
- I-94 cards for yourself and each accompanying relative
- In addition, the INS will fingerprint you and each accompanying relative between the ages of 14 and 79 as proof of identity.

Temporary Protected Status

A special category exists for aliens whose countries face major political upheavals or wars. When a specific country is designated as being unsafe for its residents to return to, Temporary Protected Status (TPS) allows aliens from that nation who are already in the United States to remain here until conditions improve in their home country.

The TPS category does not lead to a permanent green card. When conditions improve in the foreigner's home country, he or she will be required to leave the United States. Family members living overseas at the time of

TPS designation may not come to the United States under a relative's Temporary Protected Status.

Filing for Temporary Protected Status

The U.S. government announces designated TPS countries in the Federal Register and provides specific directions for filing for TPS status. Once your country is put on the list, submit the following documents to the INS:

- Forms I-104, I-765 and I-821
- Two fingerprint cards for you and each accompanying relative
- Three recent photos of you and each accompanying relative
- Evidence that you were in the United States at the time your country was assigned TPS

Highlight

The U.S. government announces designated TPS countries in the Federal Register and provides specific directions for filing for TPS status.

Special green cards

Many aliens fall between the cracks of the green card categories established by the INS. The U.S. government has created additional types of green cards for those who do not fit into the standard categories. An additional 10,000 green cards have been made available to religious workers, foreign medical graduates, former U.S. government employees, Panama Canal Zone workers, former employees of an international organization, Hong Kong Consulate workers, and to those juveniles who are dependent upon U.S. courts.

Getting one of these green cards requires filing a petition and an application. The petition process varies, and is described below. The application process, which does not vary, is described at the end of this chapter.

Religious workers

You are eligible for a green card if you are a member of and have been employed by a recognized faith for at least two years. Your faith must also have operated as a non-profit organization during that period of time. This category is open only to clergy. Lay clergy and lay persons do not qualify. Members of the clergy must come to the United States to serve as ministers in their faith or to provide other services approved by their religious organization.

The petition: Submit the following documents to the INS Regional Service Center nearest your employer:

- Form I-360

- A letter from the religious organization hiring you. This letter should describe the organization's mission, your job in the United States and the organization's method of payment.

- Proof that your religious organization is tax-exempt
- Written proof that you have been a member and employee of your faith for at least two years
- Your educational transcript(s) proving your qualifications

Foreign medical graduates

If, as a graduate of a foreign medical school, you entered the United States on an H or J visa before January 10, 1978, you are eligible for a green card. For more information about this category, contact your local INS office.

Former employees of the U.S. government

If you have worked overseas for the U.S. government for at least 15 years, you qualify for this green card. You must, however, be recommended by a prominent official from your office, and this recommendation must, in turn, be approved by the office of the Secretary of State of the United States.

The petition: Submit the following documents to your nearest INS Regional Service Center:

- Proof that you were employed overseas for at least 15 years by a U.S. government office
- A letter from a prominent official from your office recommending you for a green card
- A letter of approval from the office of the Secretary of State of the United States

Panama Canal Zone workers

If you are a Panama Canal Zone worker and wish to apply for a green card, you must have lived in the Panama Canal Zone as of April 1, 1979. You must have worked for at least one year beginning October 1, 1979, for either the Panama Canal Company or the Canal Zone government.

If you are a Panamanian native who has worked for the U.S. government in the Canal Zone for at least 15 years, you may also be eligible for this green card. You do not need a recommendation from your employer or need to meet the residency requirement. A total of 5,000 green cards are available in this category.

Highlight

If you have worked overseas for the U.S. government for at least 15 years, you qualify for this green card.

The petition: Submit the following documents to your nearest consulate or INS Regional Service Center:

- Proof of employment as of October 1, 1979, with either the Canal Zone government or the Panama Canal Company
- Panamanian natives must show proof of at least 15 years of employment in the Canal Zone by the U.S government.
- Non-natives must show proof of residency in the Canal Zone as of April 1, 1979.

Retired employees of an international organization

These green cards are for retired employees of world organizations and their spouses who formerly held G-4 or N (NATO) visas. To qualify, you must have worked for a world organization in the United States for at least 15 years, have been physically present in the United States for the last seven years, and apply for a green card within six months of your retirement.

Unmarried children of the above retired employees who are in the United States on G-4 or N visas may also apply for green cards if they have been in the United States for at least 31/2 of the last seven years, lived in the United States for at least seven years while between the ages of five and 21, and applied for a green card before age 25. Widow(er)s of retired organization workers may apply for green cards providing they have lived in the United States on a G-4 or N visa for at least 15 years before losing a spouse.

The petition: Submit the following documents to the INS:

- Proof of residence in the United States for the last 15 years while on a G-4 or N visa
- W-2 tax forms for the past 15 years
- A letter from your employer stating the length of your employment and giving proof of your presence in the U.S. for the last seven years, and the exact date of your retirement. If your unmarried children are also applying for green cards they must also have letters from your former employer stating your position and length of service.
- A birth certificate for each child immigrating with you
- Copies of I-94 cards and passports for yourself and each accompanying relative as proof of U.S. residence for the last seven years

Hong Kong Consulate workers

A U.S. consulate employee in Hong Kong who has been employed for at least three years and faces harassment or persecution because of his or her employment may apply for a green card. He or she must receive a recommendation from the U.S. Consulate General in Hong Kong and apply before January 1, 2002. For more information about this category, contact your local INS office.

Foreign juveniles who are dependent upon U.S. courts

Foreign minors in U.S. foster care who have been declared to be dependent on a U.S. juvenile court may apply for green cards. A minor may also apply if a juvenile court has decided that it is in the minor's best interests to remain in this country permanently. A foreign minor who receives a green card under this classification will never be allowed to sponsor his or her natural or adoptive parents.

Filing for green cards for court-dependent foreign juveniles

The petition: Submit the following documents to the INS:

- A copy of a decree from a U.S. juvenile court stating that the juvenile is dependent upon that court
- Foster children must submit a letter from a U.S. juvenile court stating that they are eligible for foster care.
- Nonfoster children must submit a letter from a U.S. juvenile court stating that it is in their best interest to stay in the United States.

The application

For all the above special green cards, the application process is the same. Once your initial petition is approved, submit the following documents to the INS:

- Forms I-485, G-325 and I-765
- I-94 cards for yourself and each accompanying relative
- Proof that your petition was approved by the INS
- Birth certificates for yourself and each accompanying relative
- Copies of marriage and any previous divorce certificates for you and your accompanying spouse

Highlight

A foreign minor who receives a green card under this classification will never be allowed to sponsor his or her natural or adoptive parents.

- Proof of financial support (e.g. a written job offer, proof of your personal wealth, or proof that you have a U.S. sponsor)
- Valid passports and three recent photos of yourself and each accompanying relative
- Satisfactory medical exam reports for yourself and each accompanying relative

In addition, the INS will fingerprint you and each accompanying relative between the ages of 14 and 79 as proof of identity.

All of the special categories allow spouses and unmarried children under the age of 21 to receive green cards automatically.

10

Excludability

Some people are not allowed to enter the United States under any circumstance. As undesirables, they are excluded from becoming immigrants because of physical or mental illness, drug addiction, a criminal record, previous illegal immigration, organization memberships, lack of adequate financial support, military desertion, polygamy, child custody violations, or because they are considered a threat to the United States. Some of these exclusions can be corrected or waived; others cannot. The current list of people excluded from immigrating – and in some cases, even visiting – the United States includes:

Persons with communicable diseases

This category usually applies to those infected with tuberculosis or Acquired Immune Deficiency Syndrome (AIDS), though it may apply to any communicable disease. If you have such a disease, a waiver is available, and you may be allowed to enter the United States if each of the following three requirements is met:

1) The condition may be successfully treated in the United States.

2) You have proof that you have made arrangements for such treatment.

3) You have an immediate relative who is a U.S. citizen or green card holder.

Persons with mental illness

You are subject to excludability if your mental condition may threaten the safety of others. The INS has final say as to who belongs in this category, and will decide whether or not to waive the condition.

Drug addicts or drug traffickers

If you are addicted to drugs or have sold illegal drugs, you may not enter the United States. There is no waiver available.

Convicted criminals

If you have more than one criminal conviction you may not enter the United States. You also may not enter the United States if you have one conviction for a serious felony such as murder, drug smuggling, or torture. Lesser crimes, such as prostitution, will not be held against you if they were committed at least 15 years before you apply for a green card and if the INS is convinced that you have been rehabilitated.

Illegal aliens

You may not enter the United States if:

You have ever entered the United States illegally

You do not have the required visa or passport

You smuggled illegal aliens into the United States

You have been a stowaway

If you have been deported or have lied on application forms, you may apply for a waiver if you have relatives who are U.S. citizens or green card holders. You may also be eligible for a green card if it has been more than ten years since your last offense. Persons who did not observe appropriate visa regulations may be able to get a waiver if the INS has no objection. For the most part, the INS is very tough on former illegal aliens and does not grant re-admission easily.

Groups that persecute others

If you were or are a member of the Nazi party or any group that has persecuted others, you may not enter the United States under any circumstance. There is no waiver available.

Lack of financial support

In almost every green card category you must prove that you can support yourself financially. Unless you are very wealthy, you must prove that you have a job waiting for you. If it appears that you will have to go on pub-

Highlight

In almost every green card category you must prove that you can support yourself financially. Unless you are very wealthy, you must prove that you have a job waiting for you.

lic welfare, you will not be allowed to enter the United States. There is no waiver available.

Draft evaders and military deserters

You may not enter the United States if you fall into this category, unless you were a U.S. citizen at the time the offense took place.

Polygamists

Polygamists – persons who are married to more than one person at the same time – are forbidden to enter the United States, even if polygamy is part of their religious belief. There is no waiver available.

Child abductors

Child abductors are not allowed into the United States unless their countries have signed the Hague Convention Agreement.

Threats to the United States

If you are a terrorist, spy, saboteur, or pose a risk to the United States or its foreign policy you may not enter the United States. The only exceptions are foreign government officials and those whose activities would be legal under U.S. laws. In order to enter the United States, members of totalitarian parties must have ended their membership at least five years before applying, or they must be immediate relatives of U.S. citizens of green card holders.

Fighting the excludability rulings

If you feel you have been wrongly placed in an excludable group, or if you feel there are special circumstances that may allow you to enter the United States, consult an immigration attorney.

Applying for a waiver

Keep in mind that you may not apply for a waiver until your green card application has been rejected. Even if you are sure that you belong to an excludable group, you must first go through the filing process and be refused by the INS. Sometimes the INS will refuse you immediately; at other times it will wait until the final interview. If you suspect that you may be excludable, consult with an attorney before you apply.

Highlight

Even if you are sure that you belong to an excludable group, you must first go through the filing process and be refused by the INS.

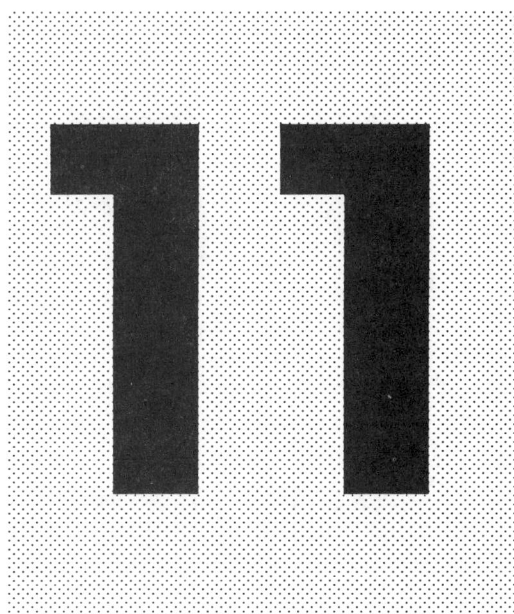

Employment and tax issues

The INS has cracked down on illegal immigration in recent years. It is not hard to understand why. There are two illegal aliens for every legal immigrant in this country. Many of these illegal aliens are working in place of those with a legal right to work.

Your right to work

The intent of the 1986 Immigration Reform Act was to discourage hiring illegal workers by requiring employers to see proof of their workers' citizenship. To prove citizenship and work legally under this law, all workers must show either a valid driver's license and Social Security card or a passport. Employers are also required to fill out an I-9 form for each new worker.

Employers must be certain not to use the above rules to discriminate against job applicants who look foreign or who have foreign-sounding names. Since an employer must see proof of citizenship, the employer may not refuse to hire an applicant simply on the suspicion that the applicant might be an illegal alien.

Employers' responsibilities

Employers hiring a foreigner on a permanent basis need to be aware of the complicated Labor Certification procedures that may be involved. Depending on the type of green card the foreign employee has, an employer must file required forms with either the central Department of Labor in Washington, D.C., or the local Department of Employment and Training. The employer may also have to provide business tax returns or other financial statements to the Department of Labor. He or she can expect to submit letters on behalf of the foreign employee explaining his or her qualifications for the job.

Strikes and wages

U.S. employers may not hire foreign workers to replace their own striking employees during a labor strike. Nor may they pay foreign workers lower wages than American employees.

Federal taxes

Both employers and foreigners should be aware of special tax rules that apply to foreign workers. The 1984 Tax Reform Act specifies that the following two groups of immigrants must pay federal taxes:

1) Green card holders must file a U.S. Tax Return Form 1040 every year by April 15. Even if they spend most of their time outside of the United States, they are responsible for paying federal income taxes.

2) Anyone spending more than six months in the United States in any one year, with or without a green card, will have to pay federal income taxes.

If you have questions about filing your tax return, consult an attorney or accountant familiar with immigration tax law.

Highlight

U.S. employers may not hire foreign workers to replace their own striking employees during a labor strike. Nor may they pay foreign workers lower wages than American employees.

12

Becoming a United States citizen

W hile a green card allows you to live and work in the United States, it does not provide you with the same rights that U.S. citizens have. As a green card holder you may not vote in elections. You also risk losing your permanent residency if you commit a crime or live outside the United States for an extended period of time.

U.S. citizenship, by contrast, is very difficult to lose. The only thing a foreign-born U.S. citizen cannot do is run for president. If you intend to remain in the United States permanently, you may want to consider applying for United States citizenship.

Naturalization

The process of becoming a U.S. citizen is called naturalization. The INS will be more likely to welcome your application if it believes that you will make a good U.S. citizen. There are 10 requirements that you must meet before you may apply for citizenship:

1) You must have entered the United States legally.

2) You must have had a green card for at least five years. However, there are exceptions to this rule:

A. The waiting period is only three years if you are the spouse of a U.S. citizen and received your green card through marriage.

B. There is no waiting period to apply for citizenship if your spouse works for the U.S. government.

C. Foreigners who served in the U.S. military, especially during World War II, may not need a green card at all before becoming naturalized citizens. Foreign veterans should consult with their home consulates.

3) You must have lived in the United States for at least 2 1/2 of the last five years, with no more than one year at a time spent outside of the United States. If you leave the United States for more than one year after receiving your green card, your five-year residency requirement will begin all over again. You also run the risk of losing your green card if the INS thinks you intend to live overseas permanently.

An exception to this rule occurs when you are working for a business firm overseas. If you file a form I-131 or form N-470 with the INS before you leave the United States, you will get credit for the time spent overseas and you will not lose your green card.

4) You must have lived in the same state for at least 90 days prior to filing your application for citizenship. If you file your application and then move to another state, you may transfer your application to the INS office in your new state. However, you must start your 90-day residency over again.

5) You must be able to read, write, and speak English. Special tutoring is available in many local high schools and community colleges. If you are over age 50 and have lived in the United States for at least 20 years, or are over the age of 55 and have lived in the United States for at least 15 years, you may be excused from the English language requirement. You must still pass the oral exam, but it will be given in your native language.

6) You must have some basic knowledge of United States history and how the United States government works. Again, there are many accredited citizenship classes given by local high schools and community colleges.

7) You must be of good moral character and be willing to uphold the principles of the United States Constitution. Under this requirement, you may be denied citizenship if:

A. You have been convicted of one or more serious criminal offenses

B. You have been sentenced to a jail term of more than 180 days

C. You failed to pay your taxes or failed to pay them on time

D. You failed to register for required military service

E. You failed to pay child support for your minor children

8) You must continue to live in the United States from the date that you file for naturalization until the day that you receive your citizenship.

9) You must intend to make the United States your permanent home.

10) You must be at least 18 years old when you file for naturalization. The only exception to this age requirement occurs when both parents of a

Highlight

You must be able to read, write, and speak English. Special tutoring is available in many local high schools and community colleges.

minor child are naturalized. The minor child will then automatically receive citizenship with the parents.

Application for naturalization

When you are within three months of fulfilling your residency requirements, you should file Form N-400 (Application for Naturalization) with the INS. Although the INS will handle your application, the final decision on any naturalization case is made by the U.S. Attorney General's office.

The INS will review your application for citizenship very carefully. The INS will compare the information that you give in your citizenship application with the information that you gave on your initial green card application. The information must be the same. If the INS discovers that you have lied, you may be deported, even after you have been given citizenship. If you think there may be something on your green card application that will cause you problems, consult an immigration attorney before you apply for citizenship.

The interview

The INS will call you for an interview within one year of receiving your application. At the interview, you will be asked to explain any discrepancies on your application. If questions remain, the INS may call you back for a second interview before making its final decision.

The examination

You will be given an oral exam at the interview. This exam will test your basic knowledge of American history and government. It is very important that you study these subjects beforehand. If you enroll in an accredited citizenship class in a local school, you will be given a test at the end of the course. If you pass that test, you do not have to take the INS test.

The questions used in the exam are available from the INS in the booklet "Guide to Naturalization Benefits," and are found in the back of this guide. Although the examining officer has the complete list of questions, he or she does not have to ask you all of them.

Common exam questions include:

What are the colors of our flag?

Who was the first president of the United States?

Highlight

If you enroll in an accredited citizenship class in a local school, you will be given a test at the end of the course. If you pass that test, you do not have to take the INS test.

How many branches are there in our government?

What is Congress?

What is the Bill of Rights?

Which countries were our enemies during World War II?

Can you name the two senators from your state?

What is the highest court in the United States?

How many times may a Senator be re-elected?

What is the introduction to the Constitution called?

If you fail the exam

You will not lose your green card if you fail the exam. While you may take the exam again in several months, this delays the naturalization process. Try to pass the exam the first time you take it.

Rejection

Once your interview and oral exam are complete, the INS will make its decision on your application within four months. If you are refused citizenship, you will be advised of your right to appeal. Often, you will be able to get your case reviewed at a U.S. District Court.

The oath of allegiance

If your application is approved, the INS will arrange for you to become a citizen through a special oath of allegiance. You will have to pledge your loyalty to the United States and, in most cases, give up your citizenship in any other country.

Dual citizenship

If your home country allows dual citizenship, however, you are allowed to pledge your loyalty to both countries. You will be allowed to retain your foreign passport in addition to receiving an American one.

Your naturalization certificate

A judge will usually administer the oath of allegiance. If a judge is unavailable, an officer from the INS will do it instead. Once you take your oath, you will be handed an official Naturalization Certificate, which makes you a citizen of the United States. You may arrange for any minor children who are becoming citizens with you to receive their own certificates by requesting their certificates at the time of your initial application. Minor children automatically become U.S. citizens at the same time that you do.

Losing your citizenship

It is very difficult to lose your U.S. citizenship once you have been naturalized. However, the two ways the government can take your citizenship away are by denaturalization and expatriation.

1) **Denaturalization:** If the INS discovers that you have lied on any of your applications, it may revoke your citizenship by bringing you to federal court and filing charges against you. If this happens, you will have 60 days to appeal. You will also be brought to court and possibly deported by the INS if you join, or refuse to testify against, any subversive group within ten years of becoming a U.S. citizen. If your children gained their citizenship through you, they may be deported when you are.

2) **Expatriation:** Any U.S. citizen can be expatriated. There are five ways to lose your citizenship through expatriation:

A. As an adult citizen, you join another country's armed forces

B. You fight against the United States

C. You give up your citizenship while the United States is at war

D. You submit a form to a Department of State consulate officer that states that you are giving up your citizenship

E. You commit any act of treason

Remember, it is not easy to lose your citizenship once you receive it. The day you receive your Naturalization Certificate will probably be one of the proudest days of your life.

Glossary
of useful terms

A

Abandonment – The desertion of a child by his parents.

Adopted orphan – Any orphan applying for a green card who has already been adopted by a U.S. citizen or green card holder.

Adoptive parents – The parents of an already adopted orphan or those parents waiting to adopt an orphan.

Advance parole – Permission given by the Immigration and Naturalization Service for an applicant to temporarily leave the United States after he or she has filed a green card application.

Affiliate – A branch of a business or a close association of two or more businesses.

Alien – A person born outside of the United States who does not have a green card and has not become a naturalized citizen.

Alien Registration Receipt Card – The official name for the green card.

Amnesty – A government pardon granted for an illegal act, such as entering the United States without permission.

Appeal – Your right to ask the court to change its decision.

Asylee – One who flees from persecution in his home country and applies for the protection of a special green card after arriving in the United States.

Asylum – Protection or safety, temporarily offered to one who is escaping from persecution in his or her home country.

Attestation – Guaranteeing that a document is genuine by signing your name as a witness. This is part of the Labor Certification process.

B-D

Bachelor's degree – The first four year college degree usually earned after graduating from high school.

Category system – There are eight main classifications of green cards. Every applicant must belong to one of these classes to receive a green card.

Child custody violator – A parent or guardian who does not act in the best interest of the child; a parent who abducts his or her child.

Citizenship – The right to live and work permanently in the United States under the full protection of the Constitution.

Citizenship class – An accredited class where you learn about U.S. history, U.S. government, and the rights and responsibilities of U.S. citizenship.

Clergy – The ordained religious leaders of a church.

Communicable disease – Any disease that can be transmitted from one person to another.

Conditional green card – A temporary green card issued for a two-year trial period.

Consulate – An office in a foreign country that represents the United States and its interests.

Criminal prosecution – Charging an individual with violating the criminal laws of the United States and attempting to prove those charges in a court of law.

Denaturalization – Canceling a person's citizenship because he or she lied on the application, because of membership in a subversive group or because of a refusal to testify against such a group.

Deportation – Cancellation of the right to live and work in the United States. The person who is deported is forced to leave and must live in a foreign country.

Diversity lottery – Randomly selecting names for green cards.

DOL – Department of Labor

Dual citizenship – Having citizenship in two separate countries at the same time.

E-H

Educational transcript – The official school record of your grades and any educational degrees you may have received.

Eligible – Meeting the requirements to be chosen for, or to fit into, a category.

Embassy – The building where the United States ambassador lives in a foreign country.

Entry visa – The document issued by a U.S. consulate or embassy giving a foreigner the right to enter the United States.

Excludability – Under this rule a condition, such as mental or physical illness or the commission of serious crimes, prevents an otherwise qualified applicant from receiving a green card.

Expatriation – The act of losing or giving up your citizenship because of treasonous activity.

Federal Register – Published daily for the general public, it contains updated information on immigration laws and regulations.

Fiance – A person engaged to be married.

Foreign passport – The official identification document of any country other than the United States.

Foreign veteran – A foreigner who served in the armed forces of the United States.

Foreigner – A person who is not a citizen of the United States.

Fraudulent marriage – A marriage arranged solely for the purpose of qualifying for a green card.

Green card – The popular name for the Alien Registration Card. A green card gives you the right to live and work permanently in the United States. A green card is also known as a permanent visa.

Home country – The country of which you are a citizen; your native country.

I-N

Illegitimate children – Children born out of wedlock.

Immigrant – A person who has received a green card and therefore is allowed to live and work in the United States permanently.

Immigration attorney – A lawyer who specializes in immigration law.

Investor green card – A class of green card issued to those foreigners willing to invest large amounts of money in a U.S. business.

INS – Immigration and Naturalization Service.

I-94 card – A card given to those whose stay in the United States is temporary. It is proof that they entered the country legally.

Job bank – A computerized list of job openings.

Joint ownership – A form of ownership in which husband and wife have an equal share in the property.

Juvenile dependent upon a U.S. court – Children who are under the protection of the court, such as foster children.

Labor Certification – A document needed by an employer before he or she is legally allowed to hire a foreign worker.

Lay clergy – Someone who does the work of a church but who has not been ordained.

Minor child – Any child under 21 years of age.

Multinational – A business having divisions in more than two countries.

Native country – See "Home country."

Naturalization – The process by which a green card holder becomes a U.S. citizen.

Naturalization certificate – The official document granting U.S. citizenship.

Non-immigrant – A person who is allowed to enter the United States for a temporary stay.

Non-immigrant visa – A document that allows a non-immigrant to enter the United States for a temporary stay, usually to visit or conduct business.

O-R

Oath of allegiance – The part of the swearing-in ceremony for new citizens wherein they promise to uphold the U.S. Constitution and give up citizenship in other countries.

Oral exam – The test given to those applying for citizenship in which questions about U.S. history and government are asked.

Orphan – A child whose parent or parents have died.

Petition – Usually the first step in the green card filing process. Specific forms are submitted by the applicant to the INS in order to receive a priority date.

Petitioner – The person, usually a relative or employer, who helps an applicant with the immigration process. Also called a sponsor.

Pre-adoption laws – Certain requirements that must be met in some states before you apply to adopt a child.

Precertified jobs – Work areas, chosen each year by the government, that do not need Labor Certification.

Preference green cards – The government's method of classifying green cards by priority. Highest priority is given to First Preference, lowest to Fourth Preference. The higher the priority, the more likely you are to receive a green card.

Preference relatives – The government's method of classifying relatives of U.S. citizens or green card holders by the green card category for which they are eligible.

Priority date – A date issued by the INS for submitting a green card application.

Quota – The limit set on the number of aliens from one classification who can enter the United States in one year.

Re-entry permit – The document that gives a green card applicant permission to return to the United States.

Refugee – One who asks to be allowed into the United States because of persecution in his or her home country.

Residency – The temporary or permanent right to live in the United States.

Rural area – The countryside, where the population is less dense than in a city.

S-W

Sibling – A brother or sister.

Sponsor – See "Petitioner."

Spouse – A husband or wife.

Status – This term usually refers to a visa, green card, or to one's citizenship. Status may be permanent, temporary, or conditional.

Stowaway – One who hides on a boat or plane to enter the United States illegally.

Tax-exempt – An employer who does not have to pay taxes.

TPS – Temporary Protection Status, offered to those already in the United States whose home countries have been identified as too dangerous to return to.

Urban area – A city.

Visa – The document issued by a U.S. consulate or embassy in a foreign country allowing an alien to enter the United States for a limited period of time.

Widow – A married woman whose husband has died.

Widower – A married man whose wife has died.

Helpful addresses

The following two organizations evaluate credentials for work-related green cards:

Educational Credential Evaluators, Inc.
P.O. Box 17499
Milwaukee, WI 53217
(414) 964-0477

Credentials Evaluation Service
International Education Research
Foundation
P.O. Box 66940
Los Angeles, CA 90066
(213) 390-6276

There are four INS Regional Service Centers:
Eastern Regional Service Center
INS
75 Lower Welden Street
St. Albans, VT 05479-0001
(802) 527-3160

Northern Regional Service Center
INS
Federal Building, U.S. Courthouse
100 Centennial Mall, N. Rm.393
Lincoln, NE 68508
(402) 437-5218

Southern Regional Service Center
INS
7701 N. Stemmons Freeway
Dallas, TX 75356
(214) 767-7769
(214) 767-7405

Western Regional Service Center
INS
24000 Avila Road
Laguna Niguel, CA 92677
(714) 643-4880
(714) 643-6122 (Fax)

Directory of local INS offices:

Alaska
INS Office
620 East 10th Avenue, Suite 102
Anchorage, AK 99501-3708
(907) 271-3449

Arizona
INS Office
2035 N. Central Avenue
Phoenix, AZ 85004
(602) 379-3114

INS Office
Federal Building
300 W. Congress, Room 1T
Tucson, AZ 85701-1386
(602) 670-5597

California
INS Office
865 Fulton Mall
Fresno, CA 93721-2816
(209) 487-5646

INS Office
300 N. Los Angeles Street
Los Angeles, CA 90012
(213) 894-2780

INS Office
711 "J" Street
Sacramento, CA 95814
(916) 551-3116

INS Office
880 Front Street
San Diego, CA 93188
(619) 428-7311

INS Office
Appraisers Building
630 Sansome Street
San Francisco, CA 94111-2280
(415) 705-4571

INS Office
280 S. First Street Rm. 1150
San Jose, CA 95113
(408) 291-7027

Colorado
INS Office
Albrook Center
4730 Paris Street
Denver, CO 80239-2804
(303) 371-0986

Connecticut
INS Office
Ribicoff Federal Building
450 Main Street
Hartford, CT 06103-3060
(203)240-3050

Florida
INS Office
400 W. Bay Street, Room G-18
Jacksonville, FL 32202
(904) 791-2624/2625

INS Office
7880 Biscayne Boulevard
Miami, FL 33138
(305) 530-7657

INS Office
4360 N. Lake Boulevard
Palm Beach Gardens, FL 33410
(407) 844-4341

INS Office
5509 W. Gray Street, Suite 113
Tampa, FL 33609
(813) 228-2165

INS Office
301 Simonton Street
Room 224, P.O. Box 86
Key West, FL 33041
(305) 296-2233/536/4274

INS Office
Fort Lauderdale/Port Everglades
1800 Eller Drive, Suite 401
P.O. Box 13054,
Port Everglades Station
Fort Lauderdale, FL 33316
(305) 356-7298/7425

Georgia
INS Office
77 Forsyth Street, S.W.
Atlanta, GA 30303
(404) 331-2788

Guam
INS Office
801 Pacific News Building
238 O'Hara Street
Agana, GU 96910
(671) 472-7253

Hawaii
INS Office
595 Ala Moana Boulevard
Honolulu, HA 96813
(808) 541-1388/89

Illinois
INS Office
10 West Jackson Boulevard, Ste 600
Chicago, IL 60604
(312) 353-7300

Indiana
INS Office
Gateway Plaza, Room 400
950 North Meridian Street
Indianapolis, IN 46204
(317) 226-7891

Kentucky
INS Office
Room 604
Gene Synder Courthouse
601 West Broadway
Lousiville, KY 40202
(502) 582-6526

Louisiana
INS Office
Postal Services Building
701 Loyola Avenue, Room T-8011
New Orleans, LA 70113
(504) 589-6521

INS Office
P.O. Box 960
Oakdale, LA 71463
(318l) 335-0713

Maine
INS Office
739 Warren Avenue
Portland, ME 04103
(207) 780-3352

Maryland
INS Office
100 South Charles St., 12th Floor
Baltimore, MD 21201
(410) 962-2010

Massachusetts
INS Office
Kennedy Federal Building
Government Center, Room 1700
Boston, MA 02203
(617) 565-4943

Michigan
INS Office
Federal Building
333 Mount Elliot Street
Detroit, MI 48207-4381
(313) 226-3250

Minnesota
INS Office
2901 Metro Drive, Suite 100
Bloomington, MN 55425
(612) 725-3456

INS Office
Bishop Henry Whipple Fed. Bldg
Room 400
One Federal Drive
Ft. Snelling, MN 55111-4007
(612) 725-3850

Missouri
INS Office
9747 N. Conant Avenue
Kansas City, MO 64153
(816)891-9314

INS Office
Robert A. Young Federal Bldg.
1222 Spruce Street
St. Louis, MO 63103-2815
(314) 539-2516

Montana
INS Office
Federal Building, Room 512
301 South Park, Drawer 10036
Helena, MT 59626
(406) 449-5220

Nebraska
INS Office
3736 S. 132nd Street
Omaha, NE 68144
(402) 697-9152

Nevada
INS Office
300 South Las Vegas Blvd.
Room 1430
Las Vegas, NV 89101
(702) 388-6640

INS Office
1351 Corporate Boulevard
Reno, NV 89502
784-5186
(702)784-5186

New Jersey
INS Office
Federal Building
970 Broad Street
Newark, NJ 07102
(201) 645-2269/2298

New Mexico
INS Office
517 Gold Avenue, S.W, Room 1010
P.O. Box 567
Albuquerque, NM 87103
(505) 766-2690

New York
INS Office
James T. Foley Federal Courthouse
Room 227
445 Broadway
Albany, NY 12207
(518) 472-7140

INS Office
68 Court Street
Buffalo, NY 14202
(716) 846-4741

INS Office
26 Federal Plaza
New York, NY 10278
(212) 264-5942

North Carolina
INS Office
6 Woodlawn Green, Room 138
Charlotte, NC 28217
(704) 371-6313

Ohio
INS Office
550 Main Street, Room 8525
Cincinnati, OH 45202
(513) 684-2939

INS Office
Anthony J. Celebreeze Federal
Building
1240 E. 9th Street, Room 1917
Cleveland, OH 44199
(216) 522-4766

Oklahoma
INS Office
4149 Highline Boulevard, Suite 300
Oklahoma City, OK 73108
(405) 231-5928

Oregon
INS Office
Federal Office Building
511 N.W. Broadway
Portland, OR 97209
(503) 326-3962

Pennsylvania
INS Office
1600 Callowhill Street
Philadelphia, PA 19130
(215) 656-7150

INS Office
2130 Federal Building
1000 Liberty Avenue
Pittsburgh, PA 15222
(412) 644-3360

Puerto Rico
INS Office
New Federal Building, 3rd Floor
Carlos Chardon Street
Hato Ray, PR 00918

INS Office
P.O. Box 365068
San Juan, PR 00936
(809) 766-5329/5380

Rhode Island
INS Office
203 John Pastore Federal Building
Providence, RI 09203
(401) 528-5315/5316

South Carolina
INS Office
Federal Building
334 Meeting Street
Charleston, SC 29403
(803) 371-6637

Tennessee
INS Office
245 Wagner Place, Suite 250
Memphis, TN 38103-3815
(901) 544-4156

Texas
INS Office
8101 N. Stemmons Freeway
Dallas, TX 75247
(214) 655-3011

INS Office
2102 Teege Road
Harlingen, TX 78550
(512) 427-8691

INS Office
509 Sam Houston Parkway
Houston, TX 77060
(713) 847-7951/7950

INS Office
Federal Building
8940 Four Winds Drive
San Antonio, TX 78239
(210) 871-7000

Utah
INS Office
230 W. 400 South Street
Salt Lake City, UT 84101
(801) 524-6272

Vermont
INS Office
Federal Building
P.O. Box 328
St. Albans, VT 05478
(802) 524-6743

INS Office
70 Kimball Avenue
South Burlington, VT 05403-6813
(802) 660-5000

Virgin Islands
INS Office
Federal Building
P.O. Box 610
Charlotte Amalie
St. Thomas, VI 00801
(809) 774-1390

Virginia
INS Office
Norfolk Federal Building
200 Granby Mall, Room 439
Norfolk, VA 23510
(804) 441-3081

Washington
INS Office
815 Airport Way, South
Seattle, WA 98134
(206) 553-0070

INS Office
691 Federal Building
Spokane, WA 99201
(509) 353-2374

Wisconsin
Federal Building, Room 186
517 E. Wisconsin Avenue
Milwaukee, WI 53202
(414) 291-3565

The forms in this guide

Note:

Although this guide contains sample forms to familiarize an applicant with the information requested, the applicant should only use original forms supplied by the INS or the DOL. In order to begin the petition or application process, the applicant should call the local INS or DOL office and request the forms by their numbers.

Instructions

Read the instructions carefully. If you do not follow the instructions, we may have to return your petition, which may delay final action. If more space is needed to complete an answer continue on separate sheet of paper.

1. Who can file?
A citizen or lawful permanent resident of the United States can file this form to establish the relationship of certain alien relatives who may wish to immigrate to the United States. You must file a separate form for each eligible relative.

2. For whom can you file?
A. If you are a citizen, you may file this form for:
1) your husband, wife, or unmarried child under 21 years old
2) your unmarried child over 21, or married child of any age
3) your brother or sister if you are at least 21 years old
4) your parent if you are at least 21 years old.
B. If you are a lawful permanent resident you may file this form for:
1) your husband or wife
2) your unmarried child
Note: If your relative qualifies under instruction A(2) or A(3) above, separate petitions are not required for his or her husband or wife or unmarried children under 21 years old. If your relative qualifies under instruction B(2) above, separate petitions are not required for his or her unmarried children under 21 years old. These persons will be able to apply for the same type of immigrant visa as your relative.

3. For whom can you not file?
You cannot file for people in the following categories:
A. An adoptive parent or adopted child, if the adoption took place after the child became 16 years old, or if the child has not been in the legal custody and living with the parent(s) for at least two years.
B. A natural parent if the United States citizen son or daughter gained permanent residence through adoption.
C. A stepparent or stepchild, if the marriage that created this relationship took place after the child became 18 years old.
D. A husband or wife, if your were not both physically present at the marriage ceremony, and the marriage was not consummated.
E. A husband or wife if you gained lawful permanent resident status by virtue of a prior marriage to a United States citizen or lawful permanent resident unless:
1) a period of five years has elapsed since you became a lawful permanent resident; OR
2) you can establish by clear and convincing evidence that the prior marriage (through which you gained your immigrant status) was not entered into for the purpose of evading any provision of the immigration laws; OR
3) your prior marriage (through which you gained your immigrant status) was terminated by the death of your former spouse.
F. A husband or wife if he or she was in exclusion, deportation, rescission, or judicial proceedings regarding his or her right to remain in the United States when the marriage took place, unless such spouse has resided outside the United States for a two-year period after the date of the marriage.
G. A husband or wife if the Attorney General · has determined that such alien has attempted or conspired to enter into a marriage for the purpose of evading the immigration laws.
H. A grandparent, grandchild, nephew, niece, uncle, aunt, cousin, or in-law.

4. What documents do your need?
You must give INS certain documents with this form to prove you are eligible to file. You must also give the INS certain documents to prove the family relationship between you and your relative.
A. For each document needed, give INS the original and one copy. However, because it is against the law to copy a Certificate of Naturalization, a Certificate of Citizenship or an Alien Registration Receipt Card (Form I-151 or I-551) give INS the original only. **Originals will be returned to you.**
B. If you do not wish to give INS the original document, you may give INS a copy. The copy must be certified by:
1) an INS or U.S. consular officer, or
2) an attorney admitted to practice law in the United States, or
3) an INS accredited representative (INS may still require originals).
C. Documents in a foreign language must be accompanied by a complete English translation. The translator must certify that the translation is accurate and that he or she is competent to translate.

5. What documents do you need to show you are a United States citizen?
A. If you were born in the United States, give INS your birth certificate.
B. If you were naturalized, give INS your original Certificate of Naturalization.
C. If you were born outside the United States, and you are a U.S. citizen through your parents, give INS:
1) your original Certificate of Citizenship, or
2) your Form FS-240 (Report of Birth Abroad of a United States Citizen).
D. In place of any of the above, you may give INS your valid unexpired U.S. passport that was initially issued for at least 5 years.
E. If you do not have any of the above and were born in the United States, see instruction under 8 below. *"What if a document is not available?"*

6. What documents do you need to show you are a permanent resident?
You must give INS your alien registration receipt card (Form I-151 or Form I-551). Do not give INS a photocopy of the card.

7. What documents do you need to prove family relationship?
You have to prove that there is a family relationship between your relative and yourself.

In any case where a marriage certificate is required, if either the husband or wife was married before, you must give INS documents to show that all previous marriages were legally ended. In cases where the names shown on the supporting documents have changed, give INS legal documents to show how the name change occurred (for example a marriage certificate, adoption decree, court order, etc.)

Find the paragraph in the following list that applies to the relative for whom you are filing.

Form I-130 (Rev. 4/11/91) Y

If you are filing for your:

A. **husband or wife,** give INS
   1) your marriage certificate
   2) a color photo of you and one of your husband or wife, taken within 30 days of the date of this petition. These photos must have a white background. They must be glossy, unretouched, and not mounted. The dimension of the facial image should be about 1 inch from chin to top of hair in 3/4 frontal view, showing the right side of the face with the right ear visible. Using pencil or felt pen, lightly print name (and Alien Registration Number, if known) on the back of each photograph.
   3) a completed and signed G-325A (Biographic Information) for you and one for your husband or wife. Except for name and signature, you do not have to repeat on the G-325A the information given on your I-130 petition.

B. **child and you are the mother,** give the child's birth certificate showing your name and the name of your child.

C. **child and you are the father or stepparent,** give the child's birth certificate showing both parents' names and your marriage certificate. **Child** born out of wedlock and you are the **father,** give proof that a parent/child relationship exists or existed. For example, the child's birth certificate showing your name and evidence that you have financially supported the child. (A blood test may be necessary).

D. **brother or sister,** your birth certificate and the birth certificate of your brother or sister showing both parents' names. If you do not have the same mother, you must also give the marriage certificates of your father to both mothers.

E. **mother,** give your birth certificate showing your name and the name of your mother.

F. **father,** give your birth certificate showing the names of both parents and your parents' marriage certificate.

G. **stepparent,** give your birth certificate showing the names of both natural parents and the marriage certificate of your parent to your stepparent.

H. **adoptive parent or adopted child,** give a certified copy of the adoption decree, the legal custody decree if you obtained custody of the child before adoption, and a statement showing the dates and places you have lived together with the child.

8. What if a document is not available?
If the documents needed above are not available, you can give INS the following instead. (INS may require a statement from the appropriate civil authority certifying that the needed document is not available.)

A. Church record: A certificate under the seal of the church where the baptism, dedication, or comparable rite occurred within two months after birth, showing the date and place of child's birth, date of the religious ceremony, and the names of the child's parents.

B. School record: A letter from the authorities of the school attended (preferably the first school), showing the date of admission to the school, child's date and place of birth, and the names and places of birth parents, if shown in the school records.

C. Census record: State or federal census record showing the names, place of birth, and date of birth or the age of the person listed.

D. Affidavits: Written statements sworn to or affirmed by two persons who were living at the time and who have personal knowledge of the event you are trying to prove; for example, the date and place of birth, marriage, or death. The persons making the affidavits need not be citizens of the United States. Each affidavit should contain the following information regarding the person making the affidavit: his or her full name, address, date and place of birth, and his or her relationship to you, if any; full information concerning the event; and complete details concerning how the person acquired knowledge of the event.

9. How should you prepare this form?
A. Type or print legibly in ink.
B. If you need extra space to complete any item, attach a continuation sheet, indicate the item number, and date and sign each sheet.
C. Answer all questions fully and accurately. If any item does not apply, please write "N/A".

10. Where should you file this form?
A. If you live in the United States, send or take the form to the INS office that has jurisdiction over where you live.
B. If you live outside the United States, contact the nearest American Consulate to find out where to send or take the completed form.

11. What is the fee?
You must pay seventy five dollars ($75.00) to file this form. **The fee will not be refunded, whether the petition is approved or not.** DO NOT MAIL CASH. All checks or money orders, whether U.S. or foreign, must be payable in U.S. currency at a financial institution in the United States. When a check is drawn on the account of a person other than yourself, write your name on the face of the check. If the check is not honored, INS will charge you $5.00.

Pay by check or money order in the exact amount. Make the check or money order payable to "Immigration and Naturalization Service". However,
A. if you live in Guam: Make the check or money order payable to "Treasurer, Guam", or
B. if you live in the U.S. Virgin Islands: Make the check or money order payable to "Commissioner of Finance of the Virgin Islands".

12. When will a visa become available?
When a petition is approved for the husband, wife, parent, or unmarried minor child of a United States citizen, these relatives do not have to wait for a visa number, as they are not subject to the immigrant visa limit. However, for a child to qualify for this category, all processing must be completed and the child must enter the United States before his or her 21st birthday.

For all other alien relatives there are only a limited number of immigrant visas each year. The visas are given out in the order in which INS receives properly filed petitions. To be considered properly filed, a petition must be completed accurately and signed, the required documents must be attached, and the fee must be paid.

For a monthly update on the dates for which immigrant visas are available, you may call (202) 647-0508.

13. What are the penalties for committing marriage fraud or submitting false information or both?
Title 8, United States Code, Section 1325 states that any individual who knowingly enters into a marriage contract for the purpose of evading any provision of the immigration laws shall be imprisoned for not more than five years, or fined not more than $250,000.00 or both.

Title 18, United States Code, Section 1001 states that whoever willfully and knowingly falsifies a material fact, makes a false statement, or makes use of a false document will be fined up to $10,000 or imprisoned up to five years, or both.

14. What is our authority for collecting this information?
We request the information on the form to carry out the immigration laws contained in Title 8, United States Code, Section 1154(a). We need this information to determine whether a person is eligible for immigration benefits. The information you provide may also be disclosed to other federal, state, local, and foreign law enforcement and regulatory agencies during the course of the investigation required by this Service. You do not have to give this information. However, if you refuse to give some or all of it, your petition may be denied.

15. Reporting Burden.
Public reporting burden for this collection of information is estimated to average 30 minutes per response, including the time for reviewing instructions, searching existing data sources, gathering and maintaining the data needed, and completing and reviewing the collection of information. Send comments regarding this burden estimate or any other aspect of this collection of information, including suggestions for reducing this burden, to: U.S. Department of Justice, Immigration and Naturalization Service (Room 5304), Washington, D.C. 20536; and to the Office of Management and Budget, Paperwork Reduction Project, OMB No. 1115-0054, Washington, D.C. 20503.

It is not possible to cover all the conditions for **eligibility** or to give instructions for every situation. If you have carefully read all the instructions and still have questions, please contact your nearest INS office.

OMB #1115-0054
Petition for Alien Relative

<table>
<tr><td colspan="3" align="center">DO NOT WRITE IN THIS BLOCK - FOR EXAMINING OFFICE ONLY</td></tr>
<tr><td>Case ID#

A#

G-28 or Volag #</td><td>Action Stamp</td><td>Fee Stamp</td></tr>
</table>

Section of Law:
- [ ] 201 (b) spouse
- [ ] 201 (b) child
- [ ] 201 (b) parent
- [ ] 203 (a)(1)
- [ ] 203 (a)(2)
- [ ] 203 (a)(4)
- [ ] 203 (a)(5)

AM CON: __________

Petition was filed on: __________________ (priority date)
- [ ] Personal Interview
- [ ] Pet. [ ] Ben. "A" File Reviewed
- [ ] Field Investigations
- [ ] 204 (a)(2)(A) Resolved
- [ ] Previously Forwarded
- [ ] Stateside Criteria
- [ ] I-485 Simultaneously
- [ ] 204 (h) Resolved

Remarks:

A. Relationship

1. **The alien relative is my**
   - [ ] Husband/Wife
   - [ ] Parent
   - [ ] Brother/Sister
   - [ ] Child

2. Are you related by adoption?
   - [ ] Yes
   - [ ] No

3. Did you gain permanent residence through adoption?
   - [ ] Yes
   - [ ] No

B. Information about you

1. **Name** (Family name in CAPS)   (First)   (Middle)

2. **Address** (Number and Street)   (Apartment Number)

   (Town or City)   (State/Country)   (ZIP/Postal Code)

3. **Place of Birth** (Town or City)   (State/Country)

4. **Date of Birth** (Mo/Day/Yr)
5. **Sex**   [ ] Male   [ ] Female
6. **Marital Status**   [ ] Married   [ ] Single   [ ] Widowed   [ ] Divorced

7. **Other Names Used** (including maiden name)

8. **Date and Place of Present Marriage** (if married)

9. **Social Security Number**
10. **Alien Registration Number** (if any)

11. **Names of Prior Husbands/Wives**
12. **Date(s) Marriages(s) Ended**

13. **If you are a U.S. citizen, complete the following:**

   My citizenship was acquired through (check one)
   - [ ] Birth in the U.S.
   - [ ] Naturalization (Give number of certificate, date and place it was issued)
   - [ ] Parents

   Have you obtained a certificate of citizenship in your own name?
   - [ ] Yes
   - [ ] No

   If "Yes", give number of certificate, date and place it was issued

14a. **If you are a lawful permanent resident alien, complete the following:**

   Date and place of admission for, or adjustment to, lawful permanent residence, and class of admission:

14b. **Did you gain permanent resident status through marriage to a United States citizen or lawful permanent resident?** [ ] Yes   [ ] No

C. Information about your alien relative

1. **Name** (Family name in CAPS)   (First)   (Middle)

2. **Address** (Number and Street)   (Apartment Number)

   (Town or City)   (State/Country)   (ZIP/Postal Code)

3. **Place of Birth** (Town or City)   (State/Country)

4. **Date of Birth** (Mo/Day/Yr)
5. **Sex**   [ ] Male   [ ] Female
6. **Marital Status**   [ ] Married   [ ] Single   [ ] Widowed   [ ] Divorced

7. **Other Names Used** (including maiden name)

8. **Date and Place of Present Marriage** (if married)

9. **Social Security Number**
10. **Alien Registration Number** (if any)

11. **Names of Prior Husbands/Wives**
12. **Date(s) Marriages(s) Ended**

13. **Has your relative ever been in the U.S.?**
   - [ ] Yes
   - [ ] No

14. **If your relative is currently in the U.S., complete the following: He or she last arrived as a** (visitor, student, stowaway, without inspection, etc.)

   Arrival/Departure Record (I-94) Number   Date arrived (Month/Day/Year)

   Date authorized stay expired, or will expire, as shown on Form I-94 or I-95

15. **Name and address of present employer** (if any)

   Date this employment began (Month/Day/Year)

16. **Has you relative ever been under immigration proceedings?**
   - [ ] Yes   [ ] No   Where __________ When __________
   - [ ] Exclusion   [ ] Deportation   [ ] Recission   [ ] Judicial Proceedings

<table>
<tr><td>INITIAL RECEIPT</td><td>RESUBMITTED</td><td colspan="2" align="center">RELOCATED</td><td colspan="3" align="center">COMPLETED</td></tr>
<tr><td></td><td></td><td>Rec'd</td><td>Sent</td><td>Approved</td><td>Denied</td><td>Returned</td></tr>
</table>

Form I-130 (Rev. 4/11/91) Y

C. (continued) Information about your alien relative

16. List husband/wife and all children of your relative (if your relative is your husband/wife, list only his or her children).

    (Name)   (Relationship)   (Date of Birth)   (Country of Birth)

17. Address in the United States where your relative intends to live

    (Number and Street)   (Town or City)   (State)

18. Your relative's address abroad

    (Number and Street)   (Town or City)   (Province)   (Country)   (Phone Number)

19. If your relative's native alphabet is other than Roman letters, write his or her name and address abroad in the native alphabet:

    (Name)   (Number and Street)   (Town or City)   (Province)   (Country)

20. If filing for your husband/wife, give last address at which you both lived together: **From**   **To**

    (Name)   (Number and Street)   (Town or City)   (Province)   (Country)   (Month)   (Year)   (Month)   (Year)

21. Check the appropriate box below and give the information required for the box you checked:

☐ Your relative will apply for a visa abroad at the American Consulate in ______________________

    (City)   (Country)

☐ Your relative is in the United States and will apply for adjustment of status to that of a lawful permanent resident in the office of the Immigration and Naturalization Service at ______________________ . If your relative is not eligible for adjustment of status, he or she will

    (City)   (State)

apply for a visa abroad at the American Consulate in ______________________ ,

    (City)   (Country)

(Designation of a consulate outside the country of your relative's last residence does not guarantee acceptance for processing by that consulate. Acceptance is at the discretion of the designated consulate.)

D. Other Information

1. If separate petitions are also being submitted for other relatives, give names of each and relationship.

2. Have you ever filed a petition for this or any other alien before?   ☐ Yes   ☐ No

If "Yes," give name, place and date of filing, and result.

Warning: The INS investigates claimed relationships and verifies the validity of documents. The INS seeks criminal prosecutions when family relationships are falsified to obtain visas.

Penalties: You may, by law be imprisoned for not more than five years, or fined $250,000, or both, for entering into a marriage contract for the purpose of evading any provision of the immigration laws and you may be fined up to $10,000 or imprisoned up to five years or both, for knowingly and willfully falsifying or concealing a material fact or using any false document in submitting this petition.

Your Certification: I certify, under penalty of perjury under the laws of the United States of America, that the foregoing is true and correct. Furthermore, I authorize the release of any information from my records which the Immigration and Naturalization Service needs to determine eligibility for the benefit that I am seeking.

Signature ______________________ Date ______________ Phone Number ______________

Signature of Person Preparing Form if Other than Above

I declare that I prepared this document at the request of the person above and that it is based on all information of which I have any knowledge.

Print Name ______________ (Address) ______________ (Signature) ______________ (Date) ______________

G-28 ID Number ______________

Volag Number ______________

NOTE: You must complete Items 1 through 6 to assure that petition approval is recorded. Do not write in the section below item 6.

1. **Name of relative** (Family name in CAPS)   (First)   (Middle)

2. **Other names used by relative** (Including maiden name)

3. **Country of relative's birth**   4. **Date of relative's birth** (Month/Day/Year)

5. **Your name** (Last name in CAPS) (First) (Middle)   6. **Your phone number**

Action Stamp

SECTION
- ☐ 201 (b)(spouse)
- ☐ 201 (b)(child)
- ☐ 201 (b)(parent)
- ☐ 203 (a)(1)
- ☐ 203 (a)(2)
- ☐ 203 (a)(4)
- ☐ 203 (a)(5)

DATE PETITION FILED

☐ **STATESIDE CRITERIA GRANTED**

SENT TO CONSUL AT;

CHECKLIST

Have you answered each question?
Have you signed the petition?
Have you enclosed:

- ☐ The filing fee for each petition?
- ☐ Proof of your citizenship or lawful permanent residence?
- ☐ All required supporting documents for each petition?

If you are filing for your husband or wife have you included:

- ☐ Your picture?
- ☐ His or her picture?
- ☐ Your G-325A?
- ☐ His or her G-325A?

Relative Petition Card
Form I-130A (Rev. 4/11/91) Y

START HERE - Please Type or Print

FOR INS USE ONLY

Part 1.   Information about you.

Family Name	Given Name	Middle Initial

Address - C/O

Street Number and Name		Apt. #
City	State or Province	
Country		ZIP/Postal Code

Date of Birth (Month/Day/Year)	Country of Birth
Social Security #	A #

Part 2.   Application Type (check one).

a. ☐ I am a permanent resident or conditional resident of the United States and I am applying for a Reentry Permit.

b. ☐ I now hold U.S. refugee or asylee status and I am applying for a Refugee Travel Document.

c. ☐ I am a permanent resident as a direct result of refugee or asylee status, and am applying for a Refugee Travel Document.

d. ☐ I am applying for an Advance Parole to allow me to return to the U.S. after temporary foreign travel.

e. ☐ I am outside the U.S. and am applying for an Advance Parole.

f. ☐ I am applying for an Advance Parole for another person who is outside the U.S. *Give the following information about that person:*

Family Name	Given Name	Middle Initial
Date of Birth (Month/Day/Year)	Country of Birth	

Foreign Address - C/O

Street Number and Name		Apt. #
City	State or Province	
Country		ZIP/Postal Code

Part 3.   Processing Information.

Date of Intended departure (Month/Day/Year)	Expected length of trip.

Are you, or any person included in this application, now in exclusion or deportation proceedings?

☐ No   ☐ Yes, at (give office name) __________________________

If applying for an Advance Parole Document, skip to Part 7.

Have you ever before been issued a Reentry Permit or Refugee Travel Document?

☐ No   ☐ Yes (give the following for the last document issued to you)

Date Issued	Disposition (attached, lost, etc.)

Form I-131 (Rev. 12/10/91) N   *Continued on back.*

FOR INS USE ONLY

Returned _______________

____

Resubmitted _______________

____

Reloc Sent _______________

____

Reloc Rec'd _______________

☐ Applicant Interviewed on
____

Receipt

Document Issued
☐ Reentry Permit
☐ Refugee Travel Document
☐ Single Advance Parole
☐ Multiple Advance Parole
Validity to __________________

If Reentry Permit or Refugee Travel Document
☐ Mail to Address in Part 2
☐ Mail to American Consulate
☐ Mail to INS overseas office
AT

Remarks:
☐ Document Hand Delivered

On   By

Action Block

To Be Completed by *Attorney* or *Representative*, if any

☐ Fill in box if G-28 is attached to represent the applicant

VOLAG#

ATTY State License #

Part 3.   Processing Information. (continued)

Where do you want this travel document sent? (check one)

a. ☐ Address in Part 2, above

b. ☐ American Consulate at (give City and Country, below)

c. ☐ INS overseas office at (give City and Country, below)

City   Country

If you checked b. or c., above, give your overseas address:

Part 4.   Information about the Proposed Travel.

Purpose of trip. *If you need more room, continue on a separate sheet of paper.*	List the countries you intend to visit.

Part 5.   Complete only if applying for a Reentry Permit.

Since becoming a Permanent Resident (or during the past five years, whichever is less) how much total time have you spent outside the United States?

☐ less than 6 months   ☐ 2 to 3 years
☐ 6 months to 1 year   ☐ 3 to 4 years
☐ 1 to 2 years   ☐ more than 4 years

Since you became a Permanent Resident, have you ever filed a federal income tax return as a nonresident, or failed to file a federal return because you considered yourself to be a nonresident? (if yes, give details on a separate sheet of paper).

☐ Yes   ☐ No

Part 6.   Complete only if applying for a Refugee Travel Document.

Country from which you are a refugee or asylee:

If you answer yes to any of the following questions, explain on a separate sheet of paper.

Do you plan to travel to the above-named country?

☐ Yes   ☐ No

Since you were accorded Refugee/Asylee status, have you ever: returned to the above-named country; applied for an/or obtained a national passport, passport renewal, or entry permit into this country; or applied for an/or received any benefit from such country (for example, health insurance benefits)?

☐ Yes   ☐ No

Since being accorded Refugee/Asylee status, have you, by any legal procedure or voluntary act, re-acquired the nationality of the above-named country, acquired a new nationality, or been granted refugee or asylee status in any other country?

☐ Yes   ☐ No

Part 7.   Complete only if applying for an Advance Parole.

On a separate sheet of paper, please explain how you qualify for an Advance Parole and what circumstances warrant issuance of Advance Parole. Include copies of any documents you wish considered. (See instructions.)

For how may trips do you intend to use this document?
If outside the U.S., at right give the U.S. Consulate or INS office you wish notified if this application is approved.

☐ 1 trip   ☐ More than 1 trip

Part 8.   Signature.   *Read the information on penalties in the instructions before completing this section. You must file this application while in the United States if filing for a reentry permit or refugee travel document.*

I certify under penalty of perjury under the laws of the United States of America that this petition, and the evidence submitted with it, is all true and correct. I authorize the release of any information from my records which the Immigration and Naturalization Service needs to determine eligibility for the benefit I am seeking.

Signature   Date   Daytime Telephone #
                                                                         (   )

Please Note: *If you do not completely fill out this form, or fail to submit required documents listed in the instructions, you may not be found eligible for the requested document and this application will have to be denied.*

Part 9.   Signature of person preparing form if other than above. (sign below)

I declare that I prepared this application at the request of the above person and it is based on all information of which I have knowledge.

Signature   Print Your Name   Date

Firm Name   Daytime Telephone #
and Address   (   )

GPO : 1994 O – 161-089

INSTRUCTIONS

Purpose of This Form.
This form is used to apply for an INS travel document, reentry permit, refugee travel document, or advance parole document. Each applicant must file a separate application.

Who May File.
Reentry permit. If you are in the United States as a permanent resident or conditional resident, you may apply for a reentry permit. A reentry permit allows a permanent resident or conditional resident to apply for admission to the U.S. during the permit's validity without having to obtain a returning resident visa from an American Consulate. A reentry permit is not required for return from a trip of less than one year's duration.

Possession of a reentry permit does not relieve you of any of the requirements of the immigration laws except the necessity to obtain a visa from an American consulate. For the purpose of later naturalization, absence from the United States for 1 year or more will normally break the continuity of any required period of continuous residence in the United States and you will need to file an application to preserve residence for naturalization purposes. Inquire at your local INS office for further information.

Refugee travel document. If you are in the United States in a valid refugee or asylee status, or obtained permanent residence as a direct result of refugee or asylee status in the U.S. you may apply for a refugee travel document. A refugee travel document is a document issued by the Service in implementation of Article 28 of the U.N. Convention of July 28, 1951. You must have a refugee travel document to return to the United States after temporary travel abroad unless you are traveling to Canada to apply for a U.S. immigrant visa (see advance parole document below).

Advance parole document. If you are outside the United States and must travel to the United States temporarily for emergent business or personal reasons, you may apply for an advance parole document to be paroled into the U.S. on humanitarian grounds if you cannot obtain the necessary visa and any required waiver of excludability. Parole cannot be used to circumvent normal visa issuing procedures, and is not a means to bypass delays in visa issuance. Parole is an extraordinary measure, sparingly used to bring an otherwise inadmissible alien into the U.S. for a temporary period of time due to a very compelling emergency.

Another person who is in the U.S. may file this application in your behalf. He or she should complete Part 1 with information about himself or herself.

If you are in the United States you may apply for an Advance Parole document if you:
- have an adjustment of status application pending which is only being held in abeyance because a visa number is not immediately available and you seek to travel abroad for bona fide business or emergent personal reasons;
- have an adjustment of status application pending for any other reason and you seek to travel abroad for emergent personal or bona fide business reasons;
- hold refugee or asylum status and intend to depart temporarily to apply for a U.S. immigrant visa in Canada; or
- seek to travel abroad temporarily for emergent personal or bona fide business reasons.

An advance parole document is issued solely to authorize the temporary parole of an individual into the United States. It may be accepted by a transportation company in lieu of a visa as authorization for the holder to travel to the United States. It is not issued to serve in lieu of any required passport.

Additional Processing Criteria.
Reentry Permit or Refugee Travel Document. A reentry permit or refugee travel document may not be issued to you if:

- you have already been issued such a document and it is still valid, unless the prior document has been returned to the Service or you can demonstrate it was lost; or
- due to national security, diplomatic or public safety reasons the government has published a notice in the Federal Register precluding issuance of such a document for travel to the area you intend to go to.

In addition, a reentry permit may not be issued if you have been a permanent resident for more than 5 years and have been outside the U.S. for more than 4 of the last 5 years, unless you are a crewman regularly serving abroad on an aircraft or vessel of American registry and the travel is in connection with your duties as a crewman,or your travel is on the orders of the United States government, other than exclusion or deportation order.)

Advance Parole. An advance parole may not be issued to a person who is in deportation proceedings, is the beneficiary of a private bill, or is subject to the 2 year foreign residence requirement due to having held J-1 nonimmigrant status.

General Filing Instructions.
Please answer all questions by typing or clearly printing in black ink. Indicate that an item is not applicable with "N/A". If an answer is "none," please so state. If you need extra space to answer any item, attach a sheet of paper with your name and your A#, if any, and indicate the number of the item. Every application must be properly signed and filed with the correct fee. You must file your application with the required Initial Evidence. If you are under 14 years of age, your parent or guardian may sign the application in your behalf.

A reentry permit or refugee travel document may be sent to a U.S. Consulate or INS office overseas for you to pick up if you request it when you file your application. However, you must be in the U.S. when you file the application.

Initial Evidence.
Evidence of eligibility. If you are a permanent resident or conditional resident, you must attach:
- a copy of your alien registration receipt card; or
- if you have not yet received your alien registration receipt card, a copy of the biographic page and the page indicating initial admission as a permanent resident of your passport, or other evidence that you are a permanent resident; or
- a copy of the approval notice of a separate application for replacement of your alien registration receipt card or temporary evidence of permanent resident status.

If you are a refugee or asylee applying for a refugee travel document, you must attach a copy of the document issued to you by the Service showing your refugee or asylee status and indicating the expiration of such status.

If you are in the U.S. and are applying for an advance parole document for yourself you must attach a copy of any document for yourself issued by the Service showing any present status in the United States, and an explanation or other evidence demonstrating the circumstances that warrant issuance of advance parole. If you are basing your eligibility for advance parole on your separate application for adjustment of status, you must also attach a copy of the filing receipt for that application. If you are traveling to Canada to apply for an immigrant visa, you must also attach a copy of the consular appointment.

If the person to be paroled is outside the U.S., you must also submit:
- a statement of how, and by whom, medical care, housing, transportation, and other expenses and subsistence need will be met;
- an Affidavit of Support (Form I-134), with evidence of the sponsor's occupation and ability to provide necessary support;

- a statement of why a U.S. visa cannot be obtained, including when and where attempts were made to obtain a visa;
- a statement of why a waiver of excludability cannot be obtained to allow issuance of a visa, including when and where attempts were made to obtain a waiver, and a copy of any written decision;
- a copy of any decision on an immigrant petition filed for the person, and evidence regarding any pending immigrant petition; and
- a complete description of the emergent reasons why parole should be authorized and copies of any evidence you wish considered, and indicating the length of time for which parole is requested.

Photographs. You must submit 2 identical natural color photographs of yourself taken within 30 days of this application. The photos must have a white background, be unmounted, printed on thin paper, and be glossy and unretouched. They should show a three-quarter frontal profile showing the right side of your face, with your right ear visible and with your head bare (unless you are wearing a headdress as required by a religious order of which you are a member). The photos should be no larger than 2 X 2 inches, with the distance from the top of the head to just below the chin about 1 and 1/4 inches. Lightly print your A# on the back of each photo with a pencil. (If you are applying for an advance parole and are outside the U.S., keep these photographs. You will be instructed as to where to submit them if parole is approved. If you are applying for parole for another person, the required photographs are of the person to be paroled.)

Copies. If these instructions state that a copy of a document may be filed with this application and you choose to send us the original, we may keep that original for our records.

Where to File.
Reentry Permit or Refugee Travel Document. Mail your application to: USINS, Northern Service Center, 100 Centennial Mall North, Room B-26, Lincoln, NE 68508.

Advance Parole. If the person being filed for is in the United States, file the application at the INS office with jurisdiction over the area in which you live. If he or she is not in the United States, mail it to: USINS, Office of International Affairs and Parole, 425 I Street N.W., Room 1203, Washington, DC 20536.

Effect of Travel Before the Travel Document is Issued.
Departure from the United States before a decision is made on an application for a reentry permit or refugee travel document does not affect the application. Departure from the United States or application for admission to the United States before a decision is made on an application for an advance parole document shall be deemed an abandonment of the application.

Fee.
The fee for this application is $65.00. The fee must be submitted in the exact amount. It cannot be refunded. DO NOT MAIL CASH. All checks and money orders must be drawn on a bank or other institution located in the United States and must be payable in United States currency. The check or money order should be made payable to the Immigration and Naturalization Service, except that:
- If you live in Guam, and are filing this application in Guam, make your check or money order payable to the "Treasurer, Guam."
- If you live in the Virgin Islands, and are filing this application in the Virgin Islands, make your check or money order payable to the "Commissioner of Finance of the Virgin Islands."

Checks are accepted subject to collection. An uncollected check will render the application and any document issued invalid. A charge of $5.00 will be imposed if a check in payment of a fee is not honored by the bank on which it is drawn.

Processing Information.
Acceptance. Any application that is not signed or is not accompanied by the correct fee will be rejected with a notice that the application is deficient. You may correct the deficiency and resubmit the application. However, an application is not considered properly filed until it is accepted by the Service.

Initial processing. Once the application has been accepted, it will be checked for completeness, including submission of the required initial evidence. If you do not completely fill out the form, or file it without required initial evidence, you will not establish a basis for eligibility, and we may deny your application.

Requests for more information or interview. We may request more information or evidence or we may request that you appear at an INS office for an interview. We may also request that you submit the originals of any copy. We will return these originals when they are no longer required.

Decision. You will be advised of the decision on your application. If it is approved, the document will be issued.

Invalidation. Any travel document obtained by making a material false representation or concealment in this application will be invalid. A document will also be invalid if you are ordered excluded or deported. In addition, a refugee travel document will be invalid if the U.N. Convention of July 28, 1951, shall cease to apply or shall not apply to you as provided in Article 1C, D, E, or F of the Convention.

Effect of Claim to Nonresident Alien Status for Federal Income Tax Purposes.
An alien who has actually established residence in the United States after having been admitted as an immigrant or after having adjusted status to that of an immigrant, and who is considering the filing of a nonresident alien tax return or the non-filing of a tax return on the ground that he/she is a nonresident alien, should consider carefully the consequences under the immigration and naturalization laws if he/she does so.

If you take such action, you may be regarded as having abandoned residence in the United States and as having lost immigrant status under the immigration and naturalization laws. As a consequence, you may be ineligible for a visa or other document for which lawful permanent resident aliens are eligible; you may be inadmissible to the United States if you seek admission as a returning resident; and you may become ineligible for naturalization on the basis of your original entry or adjustment as an immigrant.

Penalties.
If you knowingly and willfully falsify or conceal a material fact or submit a false document with this request, we will deny the benefit you are filing for, and may deny any other immigration benefit. In addition, you will face severe penalties provided by law, and may be subject to criminal prosecution.

Privacy Act Notice.
We ask for the information on this form, and associated evidence, to determine if you have established eligibility for the immigration benefit you are filing for. Our legal right to ask for this information is in 8 USC 1203 and 1225. We may provide this information to other government agencies. Failure to provide this information, and any requested evidence, may delay a final decision or result in denial of your request.

Paperwork Reduction Act Notice.
We try to create forms and instructions that are accurate, can be easily understood, and which impose the least possible burden on you to provide us with information. Often this is difficult because some immigration laws are very complex. The estimated average time to complete and file this application is as follows: (1) 10 minutes to learn about the law and form; (2) 10 minutes to complete the form; and (3) 35 minutes to assemble and file the application, for a total estimated average of 55 minutes per application. If you have comments regarding the accuracy of this estimate, or suggestions for making this form simpler, you can write to both the Immigration and Naturalization Service, 425 I Street, N.W., Room 5304, Washington, D.C. 20536; and the Office of Management and Budget, Paperwork Reduction Project, OMB No. 1115-0005, Washington, D.C. 20503.

U. S. Department of Justice
Immigration and Naturalization Service

Affidavit of Support

(ANSWER ALL ITEMS: FILL IN WITH TYPEWRITER OR PRINT IN BLOCK LETTERS IN INK.)

I, _________________________________, *residing at* _________________________________
               (Name)   (Street and Number)

_________________________________   _________________________________
   (City)   (State)   (ZIP Code if in U.S.)   (Country)

BEING DULY SWORN DEPOSE AND SAY:

1. I was born on _____________________ at _____________________
            (Date)   (City)   (Country)

   If you are *not* a native born United States citizen, answer the following as appropriate:

    a. If a United States citizen through naturalization, give certificate of naturalization number __________

    b. If a United States citizen through parent(s) or marriage, give citizenship certificate number __________

    c. If United States citizenship was derived by some other method, attach a statement of explanation.

    d. If a lawfully admitted permanent resident of the United States, give "A" number __________

2. That I am __________ years of age and have resided in the United States since (date) __________

3. That this affidavit is executed in behalf of the following person:

Name				Sex	Age
Citizen of--(Country)		Marital Status		Relationship to Deponent	
Presently resides at--(Street and Number)		(City)	(State)		(Country)

Name of spouse and children accompanying or following to join person:

Spouse	Sex	Age	Child		Sex	Age
Child	Sex	Age	Child		Sex	Age
Child	Sex	Age	Child		Sex	Age

4. That this affidavit is made by me for the purpose of assuring the United States Government that the person(s) named in item 3 will not become a public charge in the United States.

5. That I am willing and able to receive, maintain and support the person(s) named in item 3. That I am ready and willing to deposit a bond, if necessary, to guarantee that such person(s) will not become a public charge during his or her stay in the United States, or to guarantee that the above named will maintain his or her nonimmigrant status if admitted temporarily and will depart prior to the expiration of his or her authorized stay in the United States.

6. That I understand this affidavit will be binding upon me for a period of three (3) years after entry of the person(s) named in item 3 and that the information and documentation provided by me may be made available to the Secretary of Health and Human Services and the Secretary of Agriculture, who may make it available to a public assistance agency.

7. That I am employed as, or engaged in the business of __________ with __________
                                          (Type of Business)   (Name of concern)

   at __________
    (Street and Number)   (City)   (State)   (Zip Code)

   I derive an annual income of (*if self-employed, I have attached a copy of my last income tax return or report of commercial rating concern which I certify to be true and correct to the best of my knowledge and belief. See instruction for nature of evidence of net worth to be submitted.*) $__________

   I have on deposit in savings banks in the United States $__________

   I have other personal property, the reasonable value of which is $__________

Form I-134 (Rev. 12-1-84) Y   OVER

I have stocks and bonds with the following market value, as indicated on the attached list
which I certify to be true and correct to the best of my knowledge and belief. $ ___________________
I have life insurance in the sum of $ ___________________
With a cash surrender value of $ ___________________
I own real estate valued at $ ___________________
With mortgages or other encumbrances thereon amounting to $ ___________________

Which is located at____
          (Street and Number   (City)   (State)   (Zip Code)

8. That the following persons are dependent upon me for support: *(Place an "X" in the appropriate column to indicate whether
the person named is **wholly or partially** dependent upon you for support.)*

Name of Person	Wholly Dependent	Partially Dependent	Age	Relationship to Me

9. That I have previously submitted affidavit(s) of support for the following person(s). If none, state *"None"*

          Name   Date submitted
____

____

____

10. That I have submitted visa petition(s) to the Immigration and Naturalization Service on behalf of the following person(s). If
none, state none.

          Name   Relationship   Date submitted
____

____

____

11.*(Complete this block only if the person named in item 3 will be in the United States temporarily.)*
That I ☐ do intend   ☐ do not   intend, to make specific contributions to the support of the person named in item 3. *(If you
check "do intend", indicate the exact nature and duration of the contributions. For example, if you intend to furnish room and
board, state for how long and, if money, state the amount in United States dollars and state whether it is to be given in a lump
sum, weekly, or monthly, or for how long.)*

____

____

____

OATH OR AFFIRMATION OF DEPONENT

*I acknowledge at that I have read Part III of the Instructions, Sponsor and Alien Liability, and am aware of my responsibilities as
an immigrant sponsor under the Social Security Act, as amended, and the Food Stamp Act, as amended.*

I swear (affirm) that I know the contents of this affidavit signed by me and the statements are true and correct.

Signature of deponent ____

Subscribed and sworn to (affirmed) before me this __________*day of* ____________________________ , 19__________

at ____ .*My commission expires on* __________________________

Signature of Officer Administering Oath ____________________________________ *Title* ________________________

*If affidavit prepared by other than deponent, please complete the following: I declare that this document was prepared by me at the
request of the deponent and is based on all information of which I have knowledge.*

____

(Signature)   *(Address)*   *(Date)*

U. S. Department of Justice
Immigration and Naturalization Service

Affidavit of Support

INSTRUCTIONS

I. EXECUTION OF AFFIDAVIT. A separate affidavit must be submitted for each person. You must sign the affidavit in your full, true and correct name and affirm or make it under oath. If you are **in the United States** the affidavit may be sworn or affirmed before an immigration officer without the payment of fee, or before a notary public or other officer authorized to administer oaths for general purposes, in which case the official seal or certificate of authority to administer oaths must be affixed. If you are **outside the United States** the affidavit must be sworn to or affirmed before a United States consular or immigration officer.

II. SUPPORTING EVIDENCE. The deponent must submit in duplicate evidence of income and resources, as appropriate:

A. Statement from an officer of the bank or other financial institution in which you have deposits giving the following details regarding your account:
1. Date account opened.
2. Total amount deposited for the past year.
3. Present balance.

B. Statement of your employer on business stationery, showing:
1. Date and nature of employment.
2. Salary paid.
3. Whether position is temporary or permanent.

C. If self-employed:
1. Copy of last income tax return filed or,
2. Report of commercial rating concern.

D. List containing serial numbers and denominations of bonds and name of record owner(s).

III. SPONSOR AND ALIEN LIABILITY. Effective October 1, 1980, amendments to section 1614(f) of the Social Security Act and Part A of Title XVI of the Social Security Act establish certain requirements for determining the eligibility of aliens who apply for the first time for Supplemental Security Income (SSI) benefits. Effective October 1, 1981, amendments to section 415 of the Social Security Act establish similar requirements for determining the eligibility of aliens who apply for the first time for Aid to Families with Dependent Children (AFDC) benefits. Effective December 22, 1981, amendments to the Food Stamp Act of 1977 affect the eligibility of alien participation in the Food Stamp Program. These amendments require that the income and resources of any person who, as the sponsor of an alien's entry into the United States, executes an affidavit of support or similar agreement on behalf of the alien, and the income and resources of the sponsor's spouse (*if living with the sponsor*) shall be deemed to be the income and resources of the alien under formulas for determining eligibility for SSI, AFDC, and Food Stamp benefits during the three years following the alien's entry into the United States.

An alien applying for SSI must make available to the Social Security Administration documentation concerning his or her income and resources and those of the sponsor including information which was provided in support of the application for an immigrant visa or adjustment of status. An alien applying for AFDC or Food Stamps must make similar information available to the State public assistance agency. The Secretary of Health and Human Services and the Secretary of Agriculture are authorized to obtain copies of any such documentation submitted to INS or the Department of State and to release such documentation to a State public assistance agency.

Sections 1621(e) and 415(d) of the Social Security Act and subsection 5(i) of the Food Stamp Act also provide that an alien and his or her sponsor shall be jointly and severably liable to repay any SSI, AFDC, or Food Stamp benefits which are incorrectly paid because of misinformation provided by a sponsor or because of a sponsor's failure to provide information. Incorrect payments which are not repaid will be withheld from any subsequent payments for which the alien or sponsor are otherwise eligible under the Social Security Act or Food Stamp Act, except that the sponsor was without fault or where good cause existed.

These provisions do not apply to the SSI, AFDC or Food Stamp eligibility of aliens admitted as refugees, granted political asylum by the Attorney General, or Cuban/Haitian entrants as defined in section 501(e) of P.L. 96-422 and of dependent children of the sponsor or sponsor's spouse. They also do not apply to the SSI or Food Stamp eligibility of an alien who becomes blind or disabled after admission into the United States for permanent residency.

IV. AUTHORITY/USE/PENALTIES. Authority for the collection of the information requested on this form is contained in 8 U.S.C. 1182(a)(15), 1184(a), and 1258. The information will be used principally by the Service, or by any consular officer to whom it may be furnished, to support an alien's application for benefits under the Immigration and Nationality Act and specifically the assertion that he or she has adequate means of financial support and will not become a public charge. Submission of the information is voluntary. It may also, as a matter of routine use, be disclosed to other federal, state, local and foreign law enforcement and regulatory agencies, including the Department of Health and Human Services, the Department of Agriculture, the Department of State, the Department of Defense and any component thereof (if the deponent has served or is serving in the armed forces of the United States), the Central Intelligence Agency, and individuals and organizations during the course of any investigation to elicit further information required to carry out Service functions. Failure to provide the information may result in the denial of the alien's application for a visa, or his or her exclusion from the United States.

Form I-134 (Rev. 12-1-84) Y

START HERE - Please Type or Print

Part 1. Information about the person or organization filing this petition.

If an individual is filing, use the top Name line. Organizations should use the second line.

Family Name	Given Name	Middle Initial

Company or Organization

Address - Attn:

Street Number and Name	Room #

City	State or Province

Country	ZIP/Postal Code

IRS Tax #	Social Security #

Part 2. Petition Type. This petition is being filed for: (check one)

a. ☐ An alien of extraordinary ability
b. ☐ An outstanding professor or researcher
c. ☐ A multinational executive or manager
d. ☐ A member of the professions holding an advanced degree or an alien of exceptional ability
e. ☐ A skilled worker (requiring at least two years of specialized training or experience) or professional
f. ☐ An employee of a U.S. business operating in Hong Kong
g. ☐ Any other worker (requiring less than two years training or experience)

Part 3. Information about the person you are filing for.

Family Name	Given Name	Middle Initial

Address - C/O

Street # and Name	Apt. #

City	State or Province

Country	Zip or Postal Code

Date of Birth (month/day/year)	Country of Birth

Social Security # (if any)	A # (if any)

If in the U.S.	Date of Arrival (month/day/year)	I-94#
	Current Nonimmigrant Status	Expires on (month/day/year)

Part 4. Processing Information.

Below give the U.S. Consulate you want notified if this petition is approved and if any requested adjustment of status cannot be granted.

U.S Consulate: City ____________ Country ____________

Form I-140 (Rev. 12-2-91)   *Continued on back.*

FOR INS USE ONLY

Returned	Receipt
____________	
____________	
Resubmitted	
____________	
____________	
Reloc Sent	
____________	
____________	
Reloc Rec'd	
____________	
____________	

☐ Petitioner Interviewed
☐ Beneficiary Interviewed

Classification
☐ 203(b)(1)(A) Alien Of Extraordinary Ability
☐ 203(b)(1)(B) Outstanding Professor or Researcher
☐ 203(b)(1)(C) Multi-national executive or manager
☐ 203(b)(2) Member of professions w/adv. degree or of exceptional ability
☐ 203(b)(3) (A) (i) Skilled worker
☐ 203(b)(3) (A) (ii) Professional
☐ 203(b)(3) (A) (iii) Other worker
☐ Sec. 124 IMMACT-Employee of U.S. business in Hong Kong

Priority Date	Consulate

Remarks

Action Block

To Be Completed by Attorney or Representative, if any

☐ Fill in box if G-28 is attached to represent the petitioner

VOLAG#

ATTY State License #

86

Part 4.   Processing Information. *(continued)*

If you gave a U. S. address in Part 3, print the person's foreign address below. If his/her native alphabet does not use Roman letters, print his/her name and foreign address in the native alphabet.

Name   Address

Are you filing any other petitions or applications with this one?   ☐ No   ☐ yes attach an explanation
Is the person you are filing for in exclusion or deportation proceedings?   ☐ No   ☐ yes attach an explanation
Has an immigrant visa petition ever been filed by or in behalf of this person?   ☐ No   ☐ yes attach an explanation

Part 5.   Additional information about the employer.

Type of petitioner
(check one)   ☐ Self   ☐ Individual U.S. Citizen   ☐ Company or organization

                     ☐ Permanent Resident   ☐ Other explain____

If a company, give the following:
   Type of business

Date Established	Current # of employees	Gross Annual Income	Net Annual Income

If an individual, give the following:
   Occupation   Annual Income

Part 6.   Basic information about the proposed employment.

Job
Title   Nontechnical
                                                 description of job

Address where the person will work
if different from address in Part 1.

Is this a full-time
position?   ☐ yes   ☐ No (hours per week ____________)   Wages per
                                                                                   week

Is this a permanent position?:   ☐ yes   ☐ No   Is this a new position?   ☐ yes   ☐ No

Part 7.   Information on spouse and all children of the person you are filing for.

Provide an attachment listing the family members of the person you are filing for. Be sure to include their full name, relationship, date and country of birth, and present address.

Part 8.   Signature.   *Read the information on penalties in the instructions before completing this section.*

I certify under penalty of perjury under the laws of the United States of America that this petition, and the evidence submitted with it, is all true and correct.   I authorize the release of any information from my records which the Immigration and Naturalization Service needs to determine eligibility for the benefit I am seeking.

Signature   Date

Please Note: *If you do not completely fill out this form, or fail to submit required documents listed in the instructions, you cannot be found eligible for the requested document and this application may to be denied.*

Part 9.   Signature of person preparing form if other than above. *(Sign below)*

I declare that I prepared this application at the request of the above person and it is based on all information of which I have knowledge.

Signature   Print Your Name   Date

Firm Name
and Address

Purpose Of This Form.
This form is used to petition for an immigrant based on employment.

Who May File.
Any person may file this petition in behalf of an alien who:
- has extraordinary ability in the sciences, arts, education, business, or athletics, demonstrated by sustained national or international acclaim, whose achievements have been recognized in the field; or
- is claiming exceptional ability in the sciences, arts, or business, and is seeking an exemption of the requirement of a job offer in the national interest.

A U.S. employer may file this petition who wishes to employ:
- an outstanding professor or researcher, with at least 3 years of experience in teaching or research in the academic area, who is recognized internationally as outstanding,
  - in a tenured or tenure-track position at a university or institution of higher education to teach in the academic area,
  - in a comparable position at a university or institution of higher education to conduct research in the area, or
  - in a comparable position to conduct research for a private employer who employs at least 3 persons in full-time research activities and has achieved documented accomplishments in an academic field;
- an alien who, in the 3 years preceding the filing of this petition, has been employed for at least 1 year by a firm or corporation or other legal entity and who seeks to enter the U.S. to continue to render services to the same employer or to a subsidiary or affiliate in a capacity that is managerial or executive;
- a member of the professions holding an advanced degree or an alien with exceptional ability in the sciences, arts, or business who will substantially benefit the national economy, cultural or educational interests, or welfare of the U.S.;
- a skilled worker (requiring at least 2 years of specialized training or experience in the skill)- to perform labor for which qualified workers are not available in the U.S.;
- a member of the professions with a baccalaureate degree; or
- an unskilled worker to perform labor for which qualified workers are not available in the U.S.

General Filing Instructions.
Please answer all questions by typing or clearly printing in black ink. Indicate that an item is not applicable with "N/A". If an answer to a question is "none," write "none". If you need extra space to answer any item, attach a sheet of paper with your name and your A#, if any, and indicate the number of the item to which the answer refers. You must file your petition with the required Initial Evidence. Your petition must be properly signed and filed with the correct fee.

Initial Evidence.
If you are filing for an alien of extraordinary ability in the sciences, arts, education, business, or athletics, you must file your petition with:
- evidence of a one-time achievement (i.e., a major, internationally-recognized award), or
- at least three of the following:
  - receipt of lesser nationally or internationally recognized prizes or awards for excellence in the field of endeavor,
  - membership in associations in the field which require outstanding achievements as judged by recognized national or international experts,
  - published material about the alien in professional or major trade publications or other major media,
  - participation on a panel or individually as a judge of the work of others in the field or an allied field,
  - original scientific, scholarly, artistic, athletic, or business-related contributions of major significance in the field,
  - authorship of scholarly articles in the field, in professional or major trade publications or other major media,
  - display of the alien's work at artistic exhibitions or showcases,
  - evidence that the alien has performed in a leading or critical role for organizations or establishments that have a distinguished reputation,
  - evidence that the alien has commanded a high salary or other high remuneration for services, or
  - evidence of commercial successes in the performing arts, as shown by box office receipts or record, casette, compact disk, or video sales.
- If the above standards do not readily apply to the alien's occupation, you may submit comparable evidence to establish the alien's eligibility.

A U.S. employer filing for an outstanding professor or researcher must file the petition with:
- evidence of at least 2 of the following:
  - receipt of major prizes or awards for outstanding achievement in the academic field,
  - membership in associations in the academic field, which require outstanding achievements of their members,
  - published material in professional publications written by others about the alien's work in the academic field,
  - participation on a panel, or individually, as the judge of the work of others in the same or an allied academic field,
  - original scientific or scholarly research contributions to the academic field, or
  - authorship of scholarly books or articles, in scholarly journals with international circulation, in the academic field;
- evidence the beneficiary has at least 3 years of experience in teaching and/or research in the academic field; and
- if you are a university or other institution of higher education, a letter indicating that you intend to employ the beneficiary in a tenured or tenure-track position as a teacher or in a permanent position as a researcher in the academic field, or
- if you are a private employer, a letter indicating that you intend to employ the beneficiary in a permanent research position in the academic field, and evidence that you employ at least 3 full-time researchers and have achieved documented accomplishments in the field.

A U.S. employer filing for a multinational executive or manager must file the petition with a statement which demonstrates that:
- if the alien is outside the U.S., he/she has been employed outside the U.S. for at least 1 year in the past 3 years in a managerial or executive capacity by a firm or corporation or other legal entity, or by its affiliate or subsidiary; or
- if the alien is already in the U.S. working for the same employer, or a subsidiary or affiliate of the firm or corporation or other legal entity, by which the alien was employed abroad, he/she was employed by the entity abroad in a managerial or executive capacity for at least one year in the 3 years preceding his/her entry as a nonimmigrant;
  - the prospective employer in the U.S. is the same employer or a subsidiary or affiliate of the firm or corporation or other legal entity by which the alien was employed abroad;
  - the prospective U.S. employer has been doing business for at least one year; and
  - the alien is to be employed in the U.S. in a managerial or executive capacity and describing the duties to be performed.

A U.S. employer filing for a member of the professions with an advanced degree or a person with exceptional ability in the sciences, arts, or business must file the petition with:
- a labor certification (see GENERAL EVIDENCE) and either:
- an official academic record showing that the alien has a U.S. advanced degree or an equivalent foreign degree, or an official academic record showing that the alien has a U.S. baccalaureate degree or an equivalent foreign degree and letters from current or former employers showing that the alien has at least 5 years of progressive post-baccalaureate experience in the specialty; or
- at least 3 of the following:
  - an official academic record showing that the alien has a degree, diploma, certificate, or similar award from an institution of learning relating to the area of exceptional ability;
  - letters from current or former employers showing that the alien has at least 10 years of full-time experience in the occupation for which he/she is being sought;
  - a license to practice the profession or certification for a particular profession or occupation;
  - evidence that the alien has commanded a salary, or other remuneration for services, which demonstrates exceptional ability;
  - evidence of membership in professional associations; or
  - evidence of recognition for achievements and significant contributions to the industry or field by peers, governmental entities, or professional or business organizations.
- If the above standards do not readily apply to the alien's occupation, you may submit comparable evidence to establish the alien's eligibility.

A U.S. employer filing for a skilled worker must file the petition with:
- a labor certification (see GENERAL EVIDENCE); and requirement is 2 years of training or experience).
- evidence that the alien meets the educational, training, or experience and any other requirements of the labor certification (the minimum requirement is 2 years of training or experience).

A U.S. employer filing for a professional must file the petition with:
* a labor certification (see GENERAL EVIDENCE);
* evidence that the alien holds a U.S. baccalaureate degree or equivalent foreign degree; and
* evidence that a baccalaureate degree is required for entry into the occupation.

A U.S. employer filing for its employee in Hong Kong must file its petition with a statement that demonstrates that:
* the company is owned and organized in the United States
* the employee is a resident of Hong Kong;
* the company, or its subsidiary or affiliate, is employing the person in Hong Kong, and has been employing him or her there for the past 12 months, or the company, or its subsidiary or affiliate, is employing him or her outside of Hong Kong during a temporary absence (i.e., of limited duration) and he or she had been employed in Hong Kong for 12 consecutive months prior to such absence(s), and that such employment is, and for that period has been, as an officer or supervisor, or in a capacity that is executive, managerial or involves specialized knowledge;
* the company employs at least 100 employees in the U.S. and at least 50 employees outside the U.S. and has a gross annual income of at least $50,000,000; and
* the company intends to employ the person in the United States as an officer or supervisor, or in a capacity that is executive, managerial or involves specialized knowledge, with salary and benefits comparable to others with similar responsibilities and experience within the company. A specific job description is required for immediate immigration; a commitment to a qualifying job is required for deterred immigration.

A U.S. employer filing for an unskilled worker must file the petition with:
* a labor certification (see GENERAL EVIDENCE); and
* evidence that the beneficiary meets any education, training, or experience requirements required in the labor certification.

General Evidence.

Labor certification. Petitions for certain classifications must be filed with a certification from the Department of Labor or with documentation to establish that the alien qualifies for one of the shortage occupations in the Department of Labor's Labor Market Information Pilot Program or for an occupation in Group I or II of the Department of Labor's Schedule A. A certification establishes that there are not sufficient workers who are able, willing, qualified, and available at the time and place where the alien is to be employed and that employment of the alien if qualified, will not adversely affect the wages and working conditions of similarly employed U.S. workers. Application for certification is made on Form ETA-750 and is filed at the local office of the State Employment Service. If the alien is in a shortage occupation, or for a Schedule A/Group I or II occupation, you may file a fully completed, uncertified Form ETA-750 in duplicate with your petition for determination by INS that the alien belongs to the shortage occupation.

Translations. Any foreign language document must be accompanied by a full English translation which the translator has certified as complete and correct, and by the translator's certification that he or she is competent to translate from the foreign language into English.

Copies. If these instructions state that a copy of a document may be filed with this petition, and you choose to send us the original, we may keep that original for our records.

Where To File.

File this petition at the INS Service Center with jurisdiction over the place where the alien will be employed.

If the employment will be in Alabama, Connecticut, Delaware, District of Columbia, Florida, Georgia, Maine, Maryland, Massachusetts, New Hampshire, New Jersey, New York, North Carolina, Pennsylvania, Puerto Rico, Rhode Island, South Carolina, Vermont, the Virgin Islands, Virginia, or West Virginia, mail your petition to: USINS Eastern Service Center, 75 Lower Welden Street, St. Albans, VT 05479-0001.

If the employment will be in Arizona, California, Guam, Hawaii, or Nevada, mail your petition to: USINS Western Service Center, P.O. Box 30040, Laguna Niguel, CA 92607-0040.

If the employment will be elsewhere in the U.S., mail your petition to: USINS Northern Service Center, 100 Centennial Mall North, Room, B-26, Lincoln, NE 68508.

Fee.

The fee for this petition is $70.00. The fee must be submitted in the exact amount. It cannot be refunded. DO NOT MAIL CASH. All checks and money orders must be drawn on a bank or other institution located in the United States and must be payable in United States currency. The check or money order should be made payable to the Immigration and Naturalization Service, except that:
* If you live in Guam, and are filing this application in Guam, make your check or money order payable to the "Treasurer, Guam."
* If you live in the Virgin Islands, and are filing this application in the Virgin Islands, make your check or money order payable to the "Commissioner of Finance of the Virgin Islands."

Checks are accepted subject to collection. An uncollected check will render the application and any document issued invalid. A charge of $5.00 will be imposed if a check in payment of a fee is not honored by the bank on which it is drawn.

Processing Information.

Acceptance. Any petition that is not signed or is not accompanied by the correct fee will be rejected with a notice that it is deficient. You may correct the deficiency and resubmit the petition. However, a petition is not considered properly filed until accepted by the Service. A priority date will not be assigned until the petition is properly filed.

Initial processing. Once the petition has been accepted, it will be checked for completeness, including submission of the required initial evidence. If you do not completely fill out the form, or file it without required initial evidence, you will not establish a basis for eligibility, and we may deny your petition.

Requests for more information or interview. We may request more information or evidence or we may request that you appear at an INS office for an interview. We may also request that you submit the originals of any copy. We will return these originals when they are no longer required.
Decision. If you have established eligibility for the benefit requested, your petition will be approved. If you have not established eligibility, your petition will be denied. You will be notified in writing of the decision on your petition.

Meaning of petition approval.

Approval of a petition means you have established that the person you are filing for is eligible for the requested classification. This is the first step towards permanent residence. However, this does not in itself grant permanent residence or employment authorization. You will be given information about the requirements for the person to receive an immigrant visa, or to adjust status, after your petition is approved.

Penalties.

If you knowingly and willfully falsify or conceal a material fact or submit a false document with this request, we will deny the benefit you are filing for, and may deny any other immigration benefit. In addition, you will face severe penalties provided by law, and may be subject to criminal prosecution.

Privacy Act Notice.

We ask for the information on this form, and associated evidence, to determine if you have established eligibility for the immigration benefit you are filing for. Our legal right to ask for this information is in 8 USC 11854. We may provide this information to other government agencies. Failure to provide this information, and any requested evidence, may delay a final decision or result in denial of your request.

Paperwork Reduction Act Notice.

We try to create forms and instructions that are accurate, can be easily understood, and which impose the least possible burden on you to provide us with information. Often this is difficult because some immigration laws are very complex. The estimated average time to complete and file this application is as follows: (1) 20 minutes to learn about the law and form; (2) 15 minutes to complete the form; and (3) 45 minutes to assemble and file the petition; for a total estimated average of 1 hour and 20 minutes per petition. If you have comments regarding the accuracy of this estimate, or suggestions for making this form simpler, you can write to both the Immigration and Naturalization Service, 425 I Street, N.W., Room 5304, Washington, D.C. 20536; and the Office of Management and Budget, Paperwork Reduction Project, OMB No. 1115-0061, Washington, D.C. 20503.

APPLICATION FOR IMMIGRANT VISA AND ALIEN REGISTRATION

PART I – BIOGRAPHIC DATA

INSTRUCTIONS: Complete one copy of this form for yourself and each member of your family, regardless of age, who will immigrate with you. Please print or type your answer to all questions. Questions that are **Not Applicable** should be so marked. If there is insufficient room on the form, answer on a separate sheet using the same numbers as appear on the form. Attach the sheet to this form.

WARNING: Any false statement or concealment of a material fact may result in your permanent explusion from the United States.

This form (OF-230 PART I) is Part I of two parts which, together with Optional Form OF-230 PART II, constitute the complete Application for Immigrant Visa and Alien Registration.

1. FAMILY NAME	FIRST NAME	MIDDLE NAME

2. OTHER NAMES USED OR BY WHICH KNOWN *(If married woman, give maiden name)*

3. FULL NAME IN NATIVE ALPHABET *(If Roman letters not used)*

4. DATE OF BIRTH (Day) (Month) (Year)	5 AGE	6. PLACE OF BIRTH (City or town) (Province) (Country)

7. NATIONALITY *(If dual national, give both)*	8 SEX ☐ Male ☐ Female	9. MARITAL STATUS ☐ Single *(Never married)* ☐ Married ☐ Widowed ☐ Divorced ☐ Separated Including my present marriage, I have been married _______________ times.

10 PERSONAL DESCRIPTION

   a. Color of hair _______________   c Height _______________

   b. Color of eyes _______________   d. Complexion _______________

11. OCCUPATION

12. MARKS OF IDENTIFICATION

13. PRESENT ADDRESS

   Telephone number Home   Office

14. NAME OF SPOUSE *(Maiden or family name)*   *(First name)*   *(Middle name)*

Date and place of birth of spouse

Address of spouse *(If different from your own):*

15. LIST NAME, DATE AND PLACE OF BIRTH, AND ADDRESSES OF ALL CHILDREN

NAME	DATE AND PLACE OF BIRTH	ADDRESS *(If different from your own)*

APPLICATION FOR IMMIGRANT VISA AND ALIEN REGISTRATION

PART II – SWORN STATEMENT

INSTRUCTIONS: Complete one copy of this form for yourself and each member of your family, regardless of age, who will immigrate with you. Please print or type your answer to all questions. Questions that are Not Applicable should be so marked. If there is insufficient room on the form, answer on a spearate sheet using the same numbers as appear on the form. Attach the sheet to this form. DO NOT SIGN this form until instructed to do so by the consular officer. The fee for filing this application is listed under tariff item No. 20. The fee should be paid in United States dollars or local currency equivalent, or by bank draft, when you appear before the consular officer.

WARNING: Any false statement or concealment of a material fact may result in your permanent exclusion from the United States. Even though you should be admitted to the United States, a fraudulent entry could be grounds for your prosecution and/or deportation.

This form is a continuation of Form OF-230 PART I, which together, constitute the complete Application for Immigrant Visa and Alien Registration.

24. FAMILY NAME   FIRST NAME   MIDDLE NAME

25. ADDRESS (Local)

Telephone No.

26. FINAL ADDRESS TO WHICH YOU WILL TRAVEL IN THE UNITED STATES (Street address including ZIP code)

Telephone No.

27. PERSON YOU INTEND TO JOIN (Name, address, and relationship)

28. NAME AND ADDRESS OF SPONSORING PERSON OR EMPLOYER

29. PURPOSE IN GOING TO THE UNITED STATES

30. LENGTH OF INTENDED STAY (If permanently, so state)

31. INTENDED PORT OF ENTRY

32. DO YOU HAVE A TICKET TO FINAL DESTINATION?
☐ Yes   ☐ No

33. United States laws governing the issuance of visas require each applicant to state whether or not he or she is a member of any class of individuals excluded from admission into the United States. The excludable classes are described below in general terms. You should read carefully the following list and answer YES or NO to each category. The answers you give will assist the consular officer to reach a decision on your eligibility to receive a visa.

EXCEPT AS OTHERWISE PROVIDED BY LAW, ALIENS WITHIN THE FOLLOWING CLASSIFICATIONS ARE INELIGIBLE TO RECEIVE A VISA. DO ANY OF THE FOLLOWING CLASSES APPLY TO YOU?

a. An alien who has a communicable disease of public health significance, or has or has had a physical or mental disorder that poses, or is likely to pose a threat to the safety or welfare of the alien or others; an alien who is a drug abuser or addict. [212(a)(1)]   YES ☐   NO ☐

b. An alien convicted of, or who admits committing a crime involving moral turpitude, or violation of any law relating to a controlled substance; an alien convicted of 2 or more offenses for which the aggregate sentences were 5 years or more; an alien coming to the United States to engage in prostitution or commercialized vice, or who has engaged in prostitution or procuring within the past 10 years; an alien who is or has been an illicit trafficker in any controlled substance; an alien who has committed a serious criminal offense in the United States and who has asserted immunity from prosecution. [212(a)(2)]   YES ☐   NO ☐

c. Alien who seeks to enter the United States to engage in espionage, sabotage, export control violations, overthrow of the Government of the United States, or other unlawful activity; an alien who seeks to enter the United States to engage in terrorist activities; an alien who has been a member of or affiliated with the Communist or any other totalitarian party; an alien who under the direction of the Nazi government of Germany, or any area occupied by, or allied with the Nazi Government of Germany, ordered, incited, assisted, or otherwise participated in the persecution of any person because of race, religion, national origin, or political opinion; an alien who has engaged in genocide. [212(a)(3)]   YES ☐   NO ☐

d. An alien who is likely to become a public charge. [212(a)(4)]   YES ☐   NO ☐

e. An alien who seeks to enter for the purpose of performing skilled or unskilled labor who has not been certified by the Secretary of Labor; an alien graduate of a foreign medical school seeking to perform medical services who has not passed the NBME exam or its equivalent. [212(a)(5)]   YES ☐   NO ☐   Not Applicable ☐

f. An alien previously deported within one year, or arrested and deported within 5 years; an alien who seeks or has sought a visa, entry into the United States, or any U.S. immigration benefit by fraud or misrepresentation; an alien who knowingly assisted any other alien to enter or try to enter the United States in violation of the law; an alien who is in violation of Section 274C of the Immigration Act. [212(a)(6)]   YES ☐   NO ☐

THIS FORM MAY BE OBTAINED GRATIS AT CONSULAR OFFICES OF THE UNITED STATES OF AMERICA

OPTIONAL FORM 230 II (ENGLISH)
REVISED 4-91
DEPT OF STATE

PAGE 2

g. An alien who is permanently ineligible to U.S. citizenship; a person who has departed the United States to evade military service in time of war. [212(a)(8)]   YES ☐   NO ☐

h. An alien who is coming to the United States to practice polygamy; an alien who is a guardian required to accompany an excluded alien; an alien who withholds custody of a child outside the United States from a United States citizen granted legal custody. [212(a)(9)]   YES ☐   NO ☐

i. An alien who is a former exchange visitor who has not fulfilled the 2-year foreign residence requirement. [212(e)]   YES ☐   NO ☐

If the answer to any of the foregoing questions is YES or if unsure, explain in the following space or on a separate sheet of paper.

---

34. Have you ever been arrested, convicted or ever been in a prison or almshouse; have you ever been the beneficiary of a pardon or an amnesty; have you ever been treated in an institution or hospital or other place for insanity or other mental disease. [222(a)]   YES ☐   NO ☐

35. I am unlikely to become a public charge because of the following:
☐ Personal financial resources *(describe)*   ☐ Employment *(attach)*   ☐ Affidavit of Support *(attach)*

36. Have you ever applied for a visa to enter the United States?   YES ☐   NO ☐
(If answer is Yes, state where and when, whether you applied for a nonimmigrant or an immigrant visa, and whether the visa was issued or refused.)

37. Have you been refused admission to the United States?   YES ☐   NO ☐
(If answer is Yes, explain)

38. Were you assisted in completing this application?   YES ☐   NO ☐
(If answer is Yes, give name and address of person assisting you, indicating whether relative, friend, travel agent, attorney, or other)
NAME   ADDRESS   RELATIONSHIP

39. The following documents are submitted in support of this application:

☐ Passport   ☐ Military record   ☐ Evidence of own assets
☐ Birth certificate   ☐ Police certificate   ☐ Affidavit of support
☐ Marriage certificate   ☐ Medical records   ☐ Offer of employment
☐ Death certificate   ☐ Photographs   ☐ Other *(describe)*
☐ Divorce decree   ☐ Birth certificates of all children who will not be immigrating at this time. (List those for whom birth certificates are not available.)

DO NOT WRITE BELOW THE FOLLOWING LINE
The consular officer will assist you in answering Items 40 and 41.

40. I claim to be exempt from ineligibility to receive a visa and exclusion under item ______ in Part 33 for the following reasons:

212(a)(5)   Beneficiary of a Waiver under:
☐ Not Applicable   ☐ 212(a)(3)(D)(ii)   ☐ 212(e)   ☐ 212(h)
☐ Not Required   ☐ 212(a)(3)(D)(iii)   ☐ 212(g)(1)   ☐ 212(i)
☐ Attached   ☐ 212(a)(3)(D)(iv)   ☐ 212(g)(2)

41. I claim to be:
☐ A Family-Sponsored Immigrant   ☐ I derive foreign state chargeability under Sec. 202(b) through my ______
☐ An Employment Based-Immigrant
☐ A Diversity Immigrant
☐ A Special Category *(Specify)* ________________________
(Returning resident, Hong Kong, Tibetan, Private Legislation, etc.)

I am subject to the following:
☐ Preference: ______________
☐ Numerical limitation: ______________
(foreign state)

I understand that I am required to surrender my visa to the United States Immigration Officer at the place where I apply to enter the United States, and that the possession of a visa does not entitle me to enter the United States if at that time I am found to be inadmissible under the immigration laws.

I understand that any willfully false or misleading statement or willful concealment of a material fact made by me herein may subject me to permanent exclusion from the United States and, if I am admitted to the United States, may subject me to criminal prosecution and/or deportation.

I, the undersigned applicant for a United States immigrant visa, do solemnly swear (or affirm) that all statements which appear in this application, consisting of Optional Forms 230 PART I and 230 PART II combined, have been made by me, including the answers to items 1 through 41 inclusive, and that they are true and complete to the best of my knowledge and belief. I do further swear (or affirm) that, if admitted into the United States, I will not engage in activities which would be prejudicial to the public interest, or endanger the welfare, safety, or security of the United States; in activities which would be prohibited by the laws of the United States relating to espionage, sabotage, public disorder, or in other activities subversive to the national security; in any activity a purpose of which is the opposition to or the control, or overthrow of, the Government of the United States, by force, violence, or other unconstitutional means.

I understand all the foregoing statements, having asked for and obtained an explanation on every point which was not clear to me.

The relationship claimed in items 14 and 15 verified by documentation submitted to consular officer except as noted: _______________________
                                             (Signature of Applicant)

Subscribed and sworn to before me this _____ day of ____________, 19___ at: _______________________

TARIFF ITEM NO. 20.   _______________________
                                             (Consular Officer)

(Family name)	(First name)	(Middle name)	☐ MALE ☐ FEMALE	BIRTHDATE (Mo.-Day-Yr.)	NATIONALITY	FILE NUMBER A

ALL OTHER NAMES USED (Including names by previous marriages)	CITY AND COUNTRY OF BIRTH	SOCIAL SECURITY NO. (If any)

	FAMILY NAME	FIRST NAME	DATE, CITY AND COUNTRY OF BIRTH (If known)	CITY AND COUNTRY OF RESIDENCE.
FATHER				
MOTHER (Maiden name)				

HUSBAND (If none, so state) OR WIFE	FAMILY NAME (For wife, give maiden name)	FIRST NAME	BIRTHDATE	CITY & COUNTRY OF BIRTH	DATE OF MARRIAGE	PLACE OF MARRIAGE

FORMER HUSBANDS OR WIVES (If none, so state)

FAMILY NAME (For wife, give maiden name)	FIRST NAME	BIRTHDATE	DATE & PLACE OF MARRIAGE	DATE AND PLACE OF TERMINATION OF MARRIAGE

APPLICANT'S RESIDENCE LAST FIVE YEARS. LIST PRESENT ADDRESS FIRST.

STREET AND NUMBER	CITY	PROVINCE OR STATE	COUNTRY	FROM MONTH	YEAR	TO MONTH	YEAR
						PRESENT TIME	

APPLICANT'S LAST ADDRESS OUTSIDE THE UNITED STATES OF MORE THAN ONE YEAR

STREET AND NUMBER	CITY	PROVINCE OR STATE	COUNTRY	FROM MONTH	YEAR	TO MONTH	YEAR

APPLICANT'S EMPLOYMENT LAST FIVE YEARS. (IF NONE, SO STATE) LIST PRESENT EMPLOYMENT FIRST

FULL NAME AND ADDRESS OF EMPLOYER	OCCUPATION (SPECIFY)	FROM MONTH	YEAR	TO MONTH	YEAR
				PRESENT TIME	

Show below last occupation abroad if not shown above. (Include all information requested above.)

THIS FORM IS SUBMITTED IN CONNECTION WITH APPLICATION FOR:	SIGNATURE OF APPLICANT	DATE
☐ NATURALIZATION ☐ OTHER (SPECIFY): ☐ STATUS AS PERMANENT RESIDENT		
Are all copies legible? ☐ **Yes**	IF YOUR NATIVE ALPHABET IS IN OTHER THAN ROMAN LETTERS, WRITE YOUR NAME IN YOUR NATIVE ALPHABET IN THIS SPACE:	

PENALTIES: SEVERE PENALTIES ARE PROVIDED BY LAW FOR KNOWINGLY AND WILLFULLY FALSIFYING OR CONCEALING A MATERIAL FACT.

APPLICANT: BE SURE TO PUT YOUR NAME AND ALIEN REGISTRATION NUMBER IN THE BOX OUTLINED BY HEAVY BORDER BELOW.

COMPLETE THIS BOX (Family name)	(Given name)	(Middle name)	(Alien registration number)

U.S. Department of Justice
Immigration and Naturalization Service

BIOGRAPHIC INFORMATION

(Family name)	(First name)	(Middle name)	☐ MALE ☐ FEMALE	BIRTHDATE (Mo.-Day-Yr.)	NATIONALITY	FILE NUMBER A-

ALL OTHER NAMES USED (Including names by previous marriages)	CITY AND COUNTRY OF BIRTH	SOCIAL SECURITY NO. (If any)

	FAMILY NAME	FIRST NAME	DATE, CITY AND COUNTRY OF BIRTH (If known)	CITY AND COUNTRY OF RESIDENCE
FATHER				
MOTHER (Maiden name)				

HUSBAND (If none, so state) OR WIFE	FAMILY NAME (For wife, give maiden name)	FIRST NAME	BIRTHDATE	CITY & COUNTRY OF BIRTH	DATE OF MARRIAGE	PLACE OF MARRIAGE

FORMER HUSBANDS OR WIVES (if none, so state)

FAMILY NAME (For wife, give maiden name)	FIRST NAME	BIRTHDATE	DATE & PLACE OF MARRIAGE	DATE AND PLACE OF TERMINATION OF MARRIAGE

APPLICANT'S RESIDENCE LAST FIVE YEARS. LIST PRESENT ADDRESS FIRST.

STREET AND NUMBER	CITY	PROVINCE OR STATE	COUNTRY	FROM MONTH	FROM YEAR	TO MONTH	TO YEAR
						PRESENT TIME	

APPLICANT'S LAST ADDRESS OUTSIDE THE UNITED STATES OF MORE THAN ONE YEAR

STREET AND NUMBER	CITY	PROVINCE OR STATE	COUNTRY	FROM MONTH	FROM YEAR	TO MONTH	TO YEAR

APPLICANT'S EMPLOYMENT LAST FIVE YEARS. (IF NONE, SO STATE.) LIST PRESENT EMPLOYMENT FIRST

FULL NAME AND ADDRESS OF EMPLOYER	OCCUPATION (SPECIFY)	FROM MONTH	FROM YEAR	TO MONTH	TO YEAR
				PRESENT TIME	

Show below last occupation abroad if not shown above. (Include all information requested above.)

THIS FORM IS SUBMITTED IN CONNECTION WITH APPLICATION FOR:	SIGNATURE OF APPLICANT	DATE
☐ NATURALIZATION ☐ STATUS AS PERMANENT RESIDENT ☐ OTHER (SPECIFY):		

Are all copies legible? ☐ Yes	IF YOUR NATIVE ALPHABET IS IN OTHER THAN ROMAN LETTERS, WRITE YOUR NAME IN YOUR NATIVE ALPHABET IN THIS SPACE:

PENALTIES: SEVERE PENALTIES ARE PROVIDED BY LAW FOR KNOWINGLY AND WILLFULLY FALSIFYING OR CONCEALING A MATERIAL FACT.

APPLICANT: BE SURE TO PUT YOUR NAME AND ALIEN REGISTRATION NUMBER IN THE BOX OUTLINED BY HEAVY BORDER BELOW.

COMPLETE THIS BOX (Family name)	(Given name)	(Middle name)	(Ailen registration number)

Form G-325 A (Rev. 10-1-82)   (1) Ident.

START HERE - Please Type or Print

Part 1. Information about person or organization filing this petition. (Individuals should use top name line; organizations should use the second line.) *If you are filing for yourself, skip to Part 2. A widow(er) must file for him/her self.*

Family Name	Given Name	Middle Initial

Company or Organization Name

Address - C/O

Street Number and Name		Apt. #
City	State or Province	
Country	ZIP/Postal Code	

U.S. Social Security #	A #	IRS Tax # (if any)

Part 2. Classification Requested (check one):

a. ☐ Amerasian

b. ☐ Widow(er) of a U.S. citizen who died within the past 2 years

c. ☐ Special Immigrant Juvenile

d. ☐ Special Immigrant Religious Worker

e. ☐ Special Immigrant based on employment with the Panama Canal Company, Canal Zone Government or U.S. Government in the Canal Zone

f. ☐ Special Immigrant Physician

g. ☐ Special Immigrant International Organization Employee or family member

Part 3. Information about the person this petition is for.

Family Name	Given Name	Middle Initial

Address - C/O

Street Number and Name		Apt. #
City	State or Province	
Country	ZIP/Postal Code	

Date of Birth (Month/Day/Year)	Country of Birth

U.S. Social Security # (if any)	A # (if any)

Complete the items below if this person is in the United States:

Date of Arrival (Month/Day/Year)	I-94 #
Current Nonimmigrant Status	Expires on (Month/Day/Year)

FOR INS USE ONLY

Returned	Receipt
___________	
___________	
Resubmitted	
___________	
___________	
Reloc Sent	
___________	
___________	
Reloc Rec'd	
___________	
___________	

☐ Petitioner/ Applicant Interviewed

☐ Beneficiary Interviewed

☐ I-485 Filed Concurrently

☐ Bene "A" File Reviewed

Classification

Consulate

Priority Date

Remarks:

Action Block

To Be Completed by Attorney or Representative, if any

☐ Fill in box if G-28 is attached to represent the applicant

VOLAG#

ATTY State License #

Form I-360 (Rev. 09/19/91) N   *Continued on back.*

Part 4. Processing Information.

Below give the United States Consulate you want notified if this petition is approved and if any requested adjustment of status cannot be granted.

American Consulate: City	Country

If you gave a United States address in Part 3, print the person's foreign address below. If his/her native alphabet does not use Roman letters, print his/her name and foreign address in the native alphabet.

Name	Address

Sex of the person this petition is for.	☐ Male	☐ Female
Are you filing any other petitions or applications with this one?	☐ No	☐ Yes (How many? _______________)
Is the person this petition is for in exclusion or deportation proceedings?	☐ No	☐ Yes (Explain on a separate sheet of paper)
Has the person this petition is for ever worked in the U.S. without permission?	☐ No	☐ Yes (Explain on a separate sheet of paper)
Is an application for adjustment of status attached to this petition?	☐ No	☐ Yes

Part 5. Complete only if filing for an Amerasian.

Section A. Information about the mother of the Amerasian

Family Name	Given Name	Middle Initial

Living? ☐ No (Give date of death _______________) ☐ Yes (complete address line below) ☐ Unknown (attach a full explanation)

Address

Section B. Information about the father of the Amerasian: If possible, attach a notarized statement from the father regarding parentage. Explain on separate paper any question you cannot fully answer in the space provided on this form.

Family Name	Given Name	Middle Initial
Date of Birth (Month/Day/Year)	Country of Birth	

Living? ☐ No (give date of death _______________) ☐ Yes (complete address line below) ☐ Unknown (attach a full explanation)

Home Address

Home Phone #	Work Phone #

At the time the Amerasian was conceived:

☐ The father was in the military (indicate branch of service below - and give service number here): _____________________

    ☐ Army   ☐ Air Force   ☐ Navy   ☐ Marine Corps   ☐ Coast Guard

☐ The father was a civilian employed abroad. Attach a list of names and addresses of organizations which employed him at that time.

☐ If the father was not in the military, and was not a civilian employed abroad. *(Attach a full explanation of the circumstances.)*

Part 6. Complete only if filing for a Juvenile.

Section A. Information about the Juvenile

List any other names used.

Marital Status:	☐ Single	☐ Married	☐ Divorced	☐ Widowed

Answer the following questions regarding the person this petition is for. If you answer "no" explain on a separate sheet of paper.

Is he/she still a juvenile under the laws of the state in which the juvenile

court upon which the alien has been declared dependent is located?	☐ No	☐ Yes
Does he/she continue to be dependent upon the juvenile court?	☐ No	☐ Yes
Does he/she continue to be eligible for long term foster care?	☐ No	☐ Yes

Continued on next page.

Part 7. Complete only if filing for a Widow or Widower.

Section A. Information about the U.S. citizen husband or wife who died.

Family Name	Given Name	Middle Initial

Date of Birth (Month/Day/Year)	Country of Birth	Date of Death (Month/Day/Year)

His/her U.S. citizenship was based on (check one)

☐ Birth in the U.S.   ☐ Birth abroad to U.S. citizen parent(s)   ☐ Naturalization

Section B. Additional Information about you.

How many times have you been married?	How many times was the person in Section A married?

Give the date and place you and the person in Section A were married.

Did you live with this U.S. citizen spouse from the date you were married until he/she died?

☐ Yes   ☐ No (attach explanation)

Were you legally separated at the time of the United States citizen's death?

☐ Yes (attach explanation)   ☐ No

Give your address at the time of the United States citizen's death.

Part 8. Information about the children and spouse of the person this petition is for.
For a widow or widower, include any children of your deceased spouse.

	Family Name	Given Name	Middle Initial	Date of Birth (Month/Day/Year)
A.				
	Country of Birth	Relationship ☐ Spouse ☐ Child		A #
B.				
	Country of Birth	Relationship ☐ Spouse ☐ Child		A #
C.				
	Country of Birth	Relationship ☐ Spouse ☐ Child		A #
D.				
	Country of Birth	Relationship ☐ Spouse ☐ Child		A #
E.				
	Country of Birth	Relationship ☐ Spouse ☐ Child		A #
F.				
	Country of Birth	Relationship ☐ Spouse ☐ Child		A #
G.				
	Country of Birth	Relationship ☐ Spouse ☐ Child		A #
H.				
	Country of Birth	Relationship ☐ Spouse ☐ Child		A #

Continued on back.

Part 9. Signature.

I certify, or, if outside the United States, I swear or affirm, under penalty of perjury under the laws of the United States of America, that this petition, and the evidence submitted with it, is all true and correct. If filing this on behalf of an organization, I certify that I am empowered to do so by that organization. I authorize the release of any information from my records, or from the petitioning organization's records, which the Immigration and Naturalization Service needs to determine eligibility for the benefit being sought.

Signature | Date

Signature of INS or Consular Official | Print Name | Date

Please Note: *If you do not completely fill out this form, or fail to submit required documents listed in the instructions, then the person(s) filed for may not be found eligible for a requested benefit, and it may have to be denied.*

Part 10. Signature of person preparing form if other than above. (sign below)

I declare that I prepared this application at the request of the above person and it is based on all information of which I have knowledge.

Signature | Print Your Name | Date

Firm Name
and Address

INSTRUCTIONS

Purpose of This Form.

This petition is used to classify an alien as an Amerasian, Widow(er), or as a Special Immigrant (Juvenile, Religious Worker, based on employment with the Panama Canal Company, Canal Zone Government or U.S. government in the Canal Zone, Physician, International Organization Employee or family member).

Who May File; Initial Evidence Requirements.

If these instructions state that a copy of a document may be filed with this petition, and you choose to send us the original, we may keep that original for our records. Any foreign language document must be accompanied by an English translation certified by the translator that he/she is competent to translate from the foreign language into English and that the translation is accurate.

Amerasian. Any person who is 18 or older, an emancipated minor, or a U.S. corporation may file this petition for an alien who was born in Korea, Vietnam, Laos, Kampuchea, or Thailand after December 31, 1950, and before October 22, 1982, and was fathered by a U.S. citizen.

The petition must be filed with:

- copies of evidence the person this petition is for was born in one of the above countries between those dates. If he/she was born in Vietnam, you must also submit a copy of his/her Vietnamese I.D. card, or an affidavit explaining why it is not available.
- copies of evidence establishing the parentage of the person, and of evidence establishing that the biological father was a U.S. citizen. Examples of documents that may be submitted are birth or baptismal records or other religious documents; local civil records; an affidavit, correspondence or evidence of financial support from the father; photographs of the father (especially with the child); or, absent other documents, affidavits from knowledgeable witnesses which detail the parentage of the child and how they know such facts.
- a photograph of the person;
- if the person is married, submit a copy of the marriage certificate, and proof of the termination of any prior marriages;
- if the person is under 18 years old, submit a written statement from his/her mother or legal guardian which:
  - irrevocably releases him/her for emigration and authorizes the placing agencies to make necessary decisions for his/her immediate care until a sponsor receives custody;
  - shows an understanding of the effects of the release, and states whether any money was paid or coercion used prior to obtaining the release;
  - includes the full name, date and place of birth, and present or permanent address of the mother or guardian, and with the signature of the mother or guardian on the release authenticated by a local registrar, court of minors, or a U.S. immigration or consular officer.

The following sponsorship documents are also required. You may file these documents with the petition, or wait until we review the petition and request them. However, not filing them with the petition will add to the overall processing time.

- An Affidavit of Financial Support, executed by the sponsor, with the evidence of financial ability required by that form. Please note that the original sponsor remains financially responsible for the Amerasian if any subsequent sponsor fails in this area.
- Copies of evidence the sponsor is at least 21 years old and is a U.S. citizen or permanent resident.
- Fingerprints of the sponsor on Form FD-258.
- If this petition is for a person under 18 years old, the following documents issued by a placement agency must be submitted:
  - a copy of the private, public or state agency's license to place children in the U.S., proof of the agency's recent experience in the intercountry placement of children and of the agency's financial ability to arrange the placement;
  - a favorable home study of the sponsor conducted by a legally authorized agency;
  - a pre-placement report from the agency, including information regarding any family separation or dislocation abroad that would result from the placement;
  - a written description of the orientation given to the sponsor and to the parent or guardian on the legal and cultural aspects of the placement;
  - a statement from the agency showing that the sponsor has been given a report on the pre-placement screening and evaluation of the child;
  - a written plan from the agency to provide follow-up services, including mediation and counseling, and describing the contingency plans to place the person this petition is for in another suitable home if the initial placement fails.

Widow(er) of a United States Citizen. You can file this petition on your own behalf if:

- you were married for at least two years to a U.S. citizen who is now deceased and who had been a U.S. citizen for at least two years at the time of death;
- your citizen spouse's death was less than two years ago;
- you were not legally separated from your citizen spouse at the time of death, and you have not remarried.

The petition must be filed with:

- a copy of your marriage certificate to the U.S. citizen and proof of termination of any prior marriages of either of you;
- copies of evidence that your spouse was a U.S. citizen, such as a birth certificate if born in the U.S.; Naturalization Certificate or Certificate of Citizenship issued by this Service; Form FS-240, Report of Birth Abroad of a Citizen of the United States, or a U.S. passport which was valid at the time of the citizen's death;
- a copy of the death certificate of your U.S. citizen spouse.

Special Immigrant Juvenile. Any person, including the alien, can file this petition for an alien who:

- is unmarried;
- has been declared dependent upon a juvenile court in the U.S. and has been found eligible by that court for long-term foster care;
- is still a juvenile under the law of the state in which the juvenile court is located and is still dependent upon the court and eligible for long term foster care; and
- has been the subject of administrative or judicial proceedings in which it was determined that it would not be in his/her best interests to be returned to his/her country of nationality or last habitual residence, or to his/her parent's country of nationality or last habitual residence. However, after a person is admitted as a Juvenile, his/her parent may not receive any immigration benefit based on being his/her parent.

The petition must be filed with:

- copies of the court documents upon which your claim to eligibility is based.

Special Immigrant Religious Worker. Any person, including the alien, can file this petition for an alien who for the past 2 years has been a member of a religious denomination which has a bona fide nonprofit, religious organization in the U.S.; and who has been carrying on the vocation, professional work, or other work described below, continuously for the past 2 years; and seeks to enter the U.S. to work solely:

  - as a minister of that denomination; or
  - in a professional capacity in a religious vocation or occupation for that organization; or
  - in a religious vocation or occupation for the organization or its nonprofit affiliate.

A petition for a special immigrant for a person who is not a minister may only be filed until October 1, 1994.

The petition must be filed with:

- a letter from the authorized official of the religious organization establishing that the proposed services and alien qualify as above;
- a letter from the authorized official of the religious organization attesting to the alien's membership in the religious denomination and explaining, in detail, the person's religious work and all employment during the past 2 years and the proposed employment; and
- evidence establishing that the religious organization, and any affiliate which will employ the person, is a bona fide nonprofit religious organization in the U.S. and is exempt from taxation under section 501(c)(3) of the Internal Revenue Code of 1986.

Form I-360 (Rev. 09/19/91) N

Special Immigrant based on employment with the Panama Canal Company, Canal Zone Government or U.S. government in the Canal Zone. Any person can file this petition for an alien who, at the time the Panama Canal Treaty of 1977 entered into force, either:

* was resident in the Canal Zone and had been employed by the Panama Canal Company or Canal Zone Government for at least 1 year; or
* was a Panamanian national and either honorably retired from U.S. Government employment in the Canal Zone with a total of 15 or more years of faithful service or so employed for 15 years and since honorably retired; or
* was an employee of the Panama Canal Company or Canal Zone government, had performed faithful service for 5 years or more as an employee, and whose personal safety, or the personal safety of his/her spouse or child, is in danger as a direct result of the special nature of his/her employment and as a direct result of the Treaty.

The petition must be filed with:
* a letter from the Panama Canal Company, Canal Zone government or U.S. government agency employing the person in the Canal Zone, indicating the length and circumstances of employment and any retirement or termination;
* copies of evidence to establish any claim of danger to personal safety.

Special Immigrant Physician. Any person may file this petition for an alien who:
* graduated from a medical school or qualified to practice medicine in a foreign state;
* was fully and permanently licensed to practice medicine in a State of the U.S. on January 9, 1978, and was practicing medicine in a State on that date;
* entered the U.S. as an "H" or "J" nonimmigrant before January 9, 1978; and
* has been continuously present in the U.S. and continuously engaged in the practice or study of medicine since the date of such entry.

The petition must be filed with:
* letters from the person's employers, detailing his/her employment since January 8, 1978, including the current employment;
* copies of relevant documents that demonstrate that the person filed for meets all the above criteria.

Special Immigrant International Organization Employee or family member. Certain long-term "G" and "N" nonimmigrant employees of a qualifying international organization entitled to enjoy privileges, exemptions and immunities under the International Organizations Immunities Act, and certain relatives of such an employee, may be eligible to apply for classification as a Special Immigrant. To determine eligibility, contact the qualifying international organization or your local INS office. The petition must be filed with:
* a letter from the international organization demonstrating that it is a qualifying organization and explaining the circumstances of qualifying employment and the immigration status held by the person the petition is for; and
* copies of evidence documenting the relationship between the person this petition is for and the employee.

General Filing Instructions.

Please answer all questions by typing or clearly printing in black ink only. Indicate that an item is not applicable with "N/A". If an answer is "none," please so state. If you need extra space to answer any item, attach a sheet of paper with your name and your alien registration number (A#), if any, and indicate the number of the item the answer refers to. Every petition must be properly signed, and accompanied by the proper fee. If you are under 14 years of age, your parent or guardian may sign the petition.

Where to File.

If you are filing for a Special Immigrant Juvenile, file the petition at the local INS office having jurisdiction over the place he/she lives.

If you are filing for Amerasian classification and the person you are filing for is outside the United States, you may file this petition at the INS office that has jurisdiction over the place he/she lives or the office that has jurisdiction over the place he/she will live.

In all other instances file this petition at an INS Service Center, as follows:

If you live in Connecticut, Delaware, District of Columbia, Maine, Maryland, Massachusetts, New Hampshire, New Jersey, New York, Pennsylvania, Puerto Rico, Rhode Island, Vermont, Virgin Islands, Virginia, or West Virginia, mail this petition to USINS, Eastern Service Center, 75 Lower Weldon Street, St. Albans, VT 05479-0001.

If you in Alabama, Arkansas, Florida, Georgia, Kentucky, Louisiana, Mississippi, New Mexico, North Carolina, Oklahoma, South Carolina, Tennessee, or Texas, mail this petition to USINS, Southern Service Center, P.O. Box 152122, Dept. A, Irving, TX 75015-2122.

If you live in Arizona, California, Guam, Hawaii, or Nevada, mail this petition to USINS, Western Service Center, P.O. Box 30040, Laguna Niguel, CA 92607-0040

If you live elsewhere in the U.S., mail this petition to USINS, Northern Service Center, 100 Centennial Mall North, Room B-26, Lincoln, NE 68508.

Fee.

The fee for this petition is $75.00, except that there is no fee if you are filing for an Amerasian. The fee must be submitted in the exact amount. It cannot be refunded. DO NOT MAIL CASH. All checks and money orders must be drawn on a bank or other institution located in the United States and must be payable in United States currency. The check or money order should be made payable to the Immigration and Naturalization Service, except that:
* If you live in Guam, and are filing this application in Guam, make your check or money order payable to the "Treasurer, Guam."
* If you live in the Virgin Islands, and are filing this application in the Virgin Islands, make your check or money order payable to the "Commissioner of Finance of the Virgin Islands."

Checks are accepted subject to collection. An uncollected check will render the application and any document issued invalid. A charge of $5.00 will be imposed if a check in payment of a fee is not honored by the bank on which it is drawn.

Processing Information.

Rejection. Any petition that is not signed or is not accompanied by the correct fee will be rejected with a notice that the petition is deficient. You may correct the deficiency and resubmit the petition. However, a petition is not considered properly filed until accepted by the Service.

Initial processing. Once the petition has been accepted, it will be checked for completeness, including submission of the required initial evidence. If you do not completely fill out the form, or file it without required initial evidence, you will not establish a basis for eligibility and we may deny your petition.

Requests for additional information or interview. We may request additional information or evidence or we may request that you appear at an INS office for an interview. We may also request that you submit the originals of any copy. We will return these originals when they are no longer required.

Decision. If you establish that the person this petition is for is eligible for the requested classification, we will approve the petition. We will send it to the U.S. Embassy/Consulate for visa issuance unless he or she is in the U.S. and appears eligible and intends to apply for adjustment to permanent resident status while here. If you do not establish eligibility, we will deny the petition. We will notify you in writing of our decision.

Penalties.

If you knowingly and willfully falsify or conceal a material fact or submit a false document with this request, we will deny the benefit you are filing for, and may deny any other immigration benefit. In addition, you will face severe penalties provided by law, and may be subject to criminal prosecution.

Privacy Act Notice

We ask for the information on this form, and associated evidence, to determine if you have established eligibility for the immigration benefit you are filing for. Our legal right to ask for this information is in 8 USC 1154. We may provide this information to other government agencies. Failure to provide this information, and any requested evidence, may delay a final decision or result in denial of your request.

Paperwork Reduction Act Notice.

We try to create forms and instructions that are accurate, can be easily understood, and which impose the least possible burden on you to provide us with information. Often this is difficult because some immigration laws are very complex. Accordingly, the reporting burden for this collection of information is computed as follows: (1) learning about the law and form, 15 minutes; (2) completing the form, 20 minutes; and (3) assembling and filing the application, 55 minutes for an estimated average of 1 hour and 30 minutes per response. If you have comments regarding the accuracy of this estimate, or suggestions for making this form simpler, you can write to both the Immigration and Naturalization Service, 425 I Street, N.W., Room 5304, Washington, D.C. 20536; and the Office of Management and Budget, Paperwork Reduction Project, OMB No. 1115-0117, Washington, D.C. 20503.

START HERE - Please Type or Print

Part 1. Information about you.

Family Name	Given Name	Middle Initial

U.S. Mailing Address - Care of

Street Number and Name		Apt. #

City	County

State	ZIP Code

Date of Birth (month/day/year)	Country of Birth

Social Security #	A #

Part 2. Basis for Eligibility *(check one)*.

a. ☐ I have been a permanent resident for at least five (5) years .

b. ☐ I have been a permanent resident for at least three (3) years and have been married to a United States Citizen for those three years.

c. ☐ I am a permanent resident child of United States citizen parent(s) .

d. ☐ I am applying on the basis of qualifying military service in the Armed Forces of the U.S. and have attached completed Forms N-426 and G-325B

e. ☐ Other. (Please specify section of law) ________________________

Part 3. Additional information about you.

Date you became a permanent resident (month/day/year)	Port admitted with an immigrant visa or INS Office where granted adjustment of status.

Citizenship

Name on alien registration card (if different than in Part 1)

Other names used since you became a permanent resident (including maiden name)

Sex ☐ Male ☐ Female	Height	Marital Status: ☐ Single ☐ Married	☐ Divorced ☐ Widowed

Can you speak, read and write English ?   ☐No ☐Yes.

Absences from the U.S.:

Have you been absent from the U.S. since becoming a permanent resident?   ☐ No ☐Yes.

If you answered **"Yes"** , complete the following, Begin with your most recent absence. If you need more room to explain the reason for an absence or to list more trips, continue on separate paper.

Date left U.S.	Date returned	Did absence last 6 months or more?	Destination	Reason for trip
		☐ Yes ☐ No		
		☐ Yes ☐ No		
		☐ Yes ☐ No		
		☐ Yes ☐ No		
		☐ Yes ☐ No		
		☐ Yes ☐ No		

Form N-400 (Rev 07/17/91)N   *Continued on back.*

FOR INS USE ONLY

Returned	Receipt

Resubmitted

Reloc Sent

Reloc Rec'd

☐ Applicant Interviewed

At interview

☐ request naturalization ceremony at court

Remarks

Action

To Be Completed by
Attorney or Representative, if any

☐ Fill in box if G-28 is attached to represent the applicant

VOLAG#

ATTY State License #

Part 4. Information about your residences and employment.

A. List your addresses during the last five (5) years or since you became a permanent resident, whichever is less. Begin with your current address. If you need more space, continue on separate paper:

Street Number and Name, City, State, Country, and Zip Code	Dates (month/day/year)	
	From	To

B. List your employers during the last five (5) years. List your present or most recent employer first. If none, write "None". If you need more space, continue on separate paper.

Employer's Name	Employer's Address	Dates Employed (month/day/year)		Occupation/position
	Street Name and Number - City, State and ZIP Code	From	To	

Part 5. Information about your marital history.

A. Total number of times you have been married ________ . If you are now married, complete the following regarding your husband or wife.

Family name	Given name	Middle initial

Address

Date of birth (month/day/year)	Country of birth	Citizenship
Social Security#	A# (if applicable)	Immigration status (If not a U.S. citizen)

Naturalization (If applicable)
(month/day/year)   Place   (City, State)

If you have ever previously been married or if your current spouse has been previously married, please provide the following on separate paper: Name of prior spouse, date of marriage, date marriage ended, how marriage ended and immigration status of prior spouse.

Part 6. Information about your children.

B. Total Number of Children ________ . Complete the following information for each of your children. If the child lives with you, state "with me" in the address column; otherwise give city/state/country of child's current residence. If deceased, write "deceased" in the address column. If you need more space, continue on separate paper.

Full name of child	Date of birth	Country of birth	Citizenship	A - Number	Address

102

Part 7. Additional eligibility factors.

Please answer each of the following questions. If your answer is **"Yes"**, explain on a separate paper.

1. Are you now, or have you ever been a member of, or in any way connected or associated with the Communist Party, or ever knowingly aided or supported the Communist Party directly, or indirectly through another organization, group or person, or ever advocated, taught, believed in, or knowingly supported or furthered the interests of communism? ☐ Yes ☐ No

2. During the period March 23, 1933 to May 8, 1945, did you serve in, or were you in any way affiliated with, either directly or indirectly, any military unit, paramilitary unit, police unit, self-defense unit, vigilante unit, citizen unit of the Nazi party or SS, government agency or office, extermination camp, concentration camp, prisoner of war camp, prison, labor camp, detention camp or transit camp, under the control or affiliated with:

    a. The Nazi Government of Germany? ☐ Yes ☐ No

    b. Any government in any area occupied by, allied with, or established with the assistance or cooperation of, the Nazi Government of Germany? ☐ Yes ☐ No

3. Have you at any time, anywhere, ever ordered, incited, assisted, or otherwise participated in the persecution of any person because of race, religion, national origin, or political opinion? ☐ Yes ☐ No

4. Have you ever left the United States to avoid being drafted into the U.S. Armed Forces? ☐ Yes ☐ No

5. Have you ever failed to comply with Selective Service laws? ☐ Yes ☐ No
   If you have registered under the Selective Service laws, complete the following information:
   Selective Service Number:______________________ Date Registered:______________
   If you registered before 1978, also provide the following:
   Local Board Number:______________________ Classification:__________________

6. Did you ever apply for exemption from military service because of alienage, conscientious objections or other reasons? ☐ Yes ☐ No

7. Have you ever deserted from the military, air or naval forces of the United States? ☐ Yes ☐ No

8. Since becoming a permanent resident, have you ever failed to file a federal income tax return? ☐ Yes ☐ No

9. Since becoming a permanent resident, have you filed a federal income tax return as a nonresident or failed to file a federal return because you considered yourself to be a nonresident? ☐ Yes ☐ No

10 Are deportation proceedings pending against you, or have you ever been deported, or ordered deported, or have you ever applied for suspension of deportation? ☐ Yes ☐ No

11. Have you ever claimed in writing, or in any way, to be a United States citizen? ☐ Yes ☐ No

12. Have you ever:
    a. been a habitual drunkard? ☐ Yes ☐ No
    b. advocated or practiced polygamy? ☐ Yes ☐ No
    c. been a prostitute or procured anyone for prostitution? ☐ Yes ☐ No
    d. knowingly and for gain helped any alien to enter the U.S. illegally? ☐ Yes ☐ No
    e. been an illicit trafficker in narcotic drugs or marijuana? ☐ Yes ☐ No
    f. received income from illegal gambling? ☐ Yes ☐ No
    g. given false testimony for the purpose of obtaining any immigration benefit? ☐ Yes ☐ No

13. Have you ever been declared legally incompetent or have you ever been confined as a patient in a mental institution? ☐ Yes ☐ No

14. Were you born with, or have you acquired in same way, any title or order of nobility in any foreign State? ☐ Yes ☐ No

15. Have you ever:
    a. knowingly committed any crime for which you have not been arrested? ☐ Yes ☐ No
    b. been arrested, cited, charged, indicted, convicted, fined or imprisoned for breaking or violating any law or ordinance excluding traffic regulations? ☐ Yes ☐ No

(If you answer yes to 15 , in your explanation give the following information for each incident or occurrence the **city**, **state**, and **country**, where the offense took place, the **date** and **nature** of the offense, and the **outcome** or **disposition** of the case).

Part 8. Allegiance to the U.S.

If your answer to any of the following questions is **"NO"**, attach a full explanation:

1. Do you believe in the Constitution and form of government of the U.S.? ☐ Yes ☐ No
2. Are you willing to take the full Oath of Allegiance to the U.S.? (see instructions) ☐ Yes ☐ No
3. If the law requires it, are you willing to bear arms on behalf of the U.S.? ☐ Yes ☐ No
4. If the law requires it, are you willing to perform noncombatant services in the Armed Forces of the U.S.? ☐ Yes ☐ No
5. If the law requires it, are you willing to perform work of national importance under civilian direction? ☐ Yes ☐ No

Form N-400 (Rev 07/17/91)N   *Continued on back*

Part 9. Memberships and organizations.

A. List your present and past membership in or affiliation with every organization, association, fund, foundation, party, club, society, or similar group in the United States or in any other place. Include any military service in this part. If none, write "none". Include the name of organization, location, dates of membership and the nature of the organization. If additional space is needed, use separate paper.

Part 10. Complete only if you checked block " C " in Part 2.

How many of your parents are U.S. citizens? ☐ One ☐ Both (Give the following about one U.S. citizen parent:)

Family Name	Given Name	Middle Name

Address

Basis for citizenship: ☐ Birth ☐ Naturalization Cert. No.

Relationship to you (check one): ☐ natural parent ☐ adoptive parent ☐ parent of child legitimated after birth

If adopted or legitimated after birth, give date of adoption or, legitimation: (month/day/year)_______________

Does this parent have legal custody of you? ☐ Yes ☐ No

(Attach a copy of relating evidence to establish that you are the child of this U.S. citizen and evidence of this parent's citizenship.)

Part 11. Signature. *(Read the information on penalties in the instructions before completing this section).*

I certify or, if outside the United States, I swear or affirm, under penalty of perjury under the laws of the United States of America that this application, and the evidence submitted with it, is all true and correct. I authorize the release of any information from my records which the Immigration and Naturalization Service needs to determine eligibility for the benefit I am seeking.

Signature _________________________ **Date** _________

Please Note: If you do not completely fill out this form, or fail to submit required documents listed in the instructions, you may not be found eligible for naturalization and this application may be denied.

Part 12. Signature of person preparing form if other than above. *(Sign below)*

I declare that I prepared this application at the request of the above person and it is based on all information of which I have knowledge.

Signature | **Print Your Name** | **Date**

Firm Name
and Address

DO NOT COMPLETE THE FOLLOWING UNTIL INSTRUCTED TO DO SO AT THE INTERVIEW

I swear that I know the contents of this application, and supplemental pages 1 through_______, that the corrections , numbered 1 through_______, were made at my request, and that this amended application, is true to the best of my knowledge and belief.

____
(Complete and true signature of applicant)

Subscribed and sworn to before me by the applicant.

____
(Examiner's Signature)   Date

104

INSTRUCTIONS

Purpose of This Form.
This form is for use to apply to become a naturalized citizen of the United States.

Who May File.
You may apply for naturalization if:
- you have been a lawful permanent resident for five years;
- you have been a lawful permanent resident for three years, have been married to a United States citizen for those three years, and continue to be married to that U.S. citizen;
- you are the lawful permanent resident child of United States citizen parents; or
- you have qualifying military service.

Children under 18 may automatically become citizens when their parents naturalize. You may inquire at your local Service office for further information. If you do not meet the qualifications listed above but believe that you are eligible for naturalization, you may inquire at your local Service office for additional information.

General Instructions.
Please answer all questions by typing or clearly printing in black ink. Indicate that an item is not applicable with "N/A". If an answer is "none," write "none". If you need extra space to answer any item, attach a sheet of paper with your name and your alien registration number (A#), if any, and indicate the number of the item.

Every application must be properly signed and filed with the correct fee. If you are under 18 years of age, your parent or guardian must sign the application.

If you wish to be called for your examination at the same time as another person who is also applying for naturalization, make your request on a separate cover sheet. Be sure to give the name and alien registration number of that person.

Initial Evidence Requirements.
You must file your application with the following evidence:

A copy of your alien registration card.

Photographs. You must submit two color photographs of yourself taken within 30 days of this application. These photos must be glossy, unretouched and unmounted, and have a white background. Dimension of the face should be about 1 inch from chin to top of hair. Face should be 3/4 frontal view of right side with right ear visible. Using pencil or felt pen, lightly print name and A#, if any, on the back of each photo. This requirement may be waived by the Service if you can establish that you are confined because of age or physical infirmity.

Fingerprints. If you are between the ages of 14 and 75, you must sumit your fingerprints on Form FD-258. Fill out the form and write your Alien Registration Number in the space marked "Your No. OCA" or "Miscellaneous No. MNU". Take the chart and these instructions to a police station, sheriff's office or an office of this Service, or other reputable person or organization for fingerprinting. (You should contact the police or sheriff's office before going there since some of these offices do not take fingerprints for other government agencies.) You must sign the chart in the presence of the person taking your fingerprints and have that person sign his/her name, title, and the date in the space provided. Do not bend, fold, or crease the fingerprint chart.

U.S. Military Service. If you have ever served in the Armed Forces of the United States at any time, you must submit a completed Form G-325B. If your application is based on your military service you must also submit Form N-426, "Request for Certification of Military or Naval Service."

Application for Child. If this application is for a permanent resident child of U.S. citizen parents, you must also submit copies of the child's birth certificate, the parents' marriage certificate, and evidence of the parents' U.S. citizenship. If the parents are divorced, you must also submit the divorce decree and evidence that the citizen parent has legal custody of the child.

Where to File.
File this application at the local Service office having jurisdiction over your place of residence.

Fee.
The fee for this application is $90.00. The fee must be submitted in the exact amount. It cannot be refunded. DO NOT MAIL CASH.

All checks and money orders must be drawn on a bank or other institution located in the United States and must be payable in United States currency. The check or money order should be made payable to the Immigration and Naturalization Service, except that:
- If you live in Guam, and are filing this application in Guam, make your check or money order payable to the "Treasurer, Guam."
- If you live in the Virgin Islands, and are filing this application in the Virgin Islands, make your check or money order payable to the "Commissioner of Finance of the Virgin Islands."

Checks are accepted subject to collection. An uncollected check will render the application and any document issued invalid. A charge of $5.00 will be imposed if a check in payment of a fee is not honored by the bank on which it is drawn.

Form N-400 (Rev. 07/17/91) N

Processing Information.
Rejection. Any application that is not signed or is not accompanied by the proper fee will be rejected with a notice that the application is deficient. You may correct the deficiency and resubmit the application. However, an application is not considered properly filed until it is accepted by the Service.

Requests for more information. We may request more information or evidence. We may also request that you submit the originals of any copy. We will return these originals when they are no longer required.

Interview. After you file your application, you will be notified to appear at a Service office to be examined under oath or affirmation. This interview may not be waived. If you are an adult, you must show that you have a knowledge and understanding of the history, principles, and form of government of the United States. There is no exemption from this requirement.

You will also be examined on your ability to read, write, and speak English. If on the date of your examination you are more than 50 years of age and have been a lawful permanent resident for 20 years or more, or you are 55 years of age and have been a lawful permanent resident for at least 15 years, you will be exempt from the English language requirements of the law. If you are exempt, you may take the examination in any language you wish.

Oath of Allegiance. If your application is approved, you will be required to take the following oath of allegiance to the United States in order to become a citizen:

"I hereby declare, on oath, that I absolutely and entirely renounce and abjure all allegiance and fidelity to any foreign prince, potentate, state or sovereignty, of whom or which I have heretofore been a subject or citizen; that I will support and defend the Constitution and laws of the United States of America against all enemies, foreign and domestic; that I will bear true faith and allegiance to the same; that I will bear arms on behalf of the United States when required by the law; that I will perform noncombatant service in the armed forces of the United States when required by the law; that I will perform work of national importance under civilian direction when required by the law; and that I take this obligation freely without any mental reservation or purpose of evasion; so help me God."

If you cannot promise to bear arms or perform noncombatant service because of religious training and belief, you may omit those statements when taking the oath. "Religious training and belief" means a person's belief in relation to a Supreme Being involving duties superior to those arising from any human relation, but does not include essentially political, sociological, or philosophical views or merely a personal moral code.

Oath ceremony. You may choose to have the oath of allegiance administered in a ceremony conducted by the Service or request to be scheduled for an oath ceremony in a court that has jurisdiction over the applicant's place of residence. At the time of your examination you will be asked to elect either form of ceremony. You will become a citizen on the date of the oath ceremony and the Attorney General will issue a Certificate of Naturalization as evidence of United States citizenship.

If you wish to change your name as part of the naturalization process, you will have to take the oath in court.

Penalties.
If you knowingly and willfully falsify or conceal a material fact or submit a false document with this request, we will deny the benefit you are filing for, and may deny any other immigration benefit. In addition, you will face severe penalties provided by law, and may be subject to criminal prosecution.

Privacy Act Notice.
We ask for the information on this form, and associated evidence, to determine if you have established eligibility for the immigration benefit you are filing for. Our legal right to ask for this information is in 8 USC 1439, 1440, 1443, 1445, 1446, and 1452. We may provide this information to other government agencies. Failure to provide this information, and any requested evidence, may delay a final decision or result in denial of your request.

Paperwork Reduction Act Notice.
We try to create forms and instructions that are accurate, can be easily understood, and which impose the least possible burden on you to provide us with information. Often this is difficult because some immigration laws are very complex. Accordingly, the reporting burden for this collection of information is computed as follows: (1) learning about the law and form, 20 minutes; (2) completing the form, 25 minutes; and (3) assembling and filing the application (includes statutory required interview and travel time, after filing of application), 3 hours and 35 minutes, for an estimated average of 4 hours and 20 minutes per response. If you have comments regarding the accuracy of this estimate, or suggestions for making this form simpler, you can write to both the Immigration and Naturalization Service, 425 I Street, N.W., Room 5304, Washington, D.C. 20536; and the Office of Management and Budget, Paperwork Reduction Project, OMB No. 1115-0009, Washington, D.C. 20503.

Application for Permanent Residence

OMB # 1115-0053
Expires 8/85

DO NOT WRITE IN THIS BLOCK

Case ID#	Action Stamp	Fee Stamp
A#		
G-28 or Volag#		

Section of Law
- ☐ Sec. 209(b). INA
- ☐ Sec. 214(d). INA
- ☐ Sec. 13. Act of 9/11/57
- ☐ Sec. 245. INA
- ☐ Sec. 249. INA

Country Chargeable __________________

Eligibility Under Sec. 245
- ☐ Approved Visa Petition
- ☐ Dependent of Principal Alien
- ☐ Special Immigrant
- ☐ Other __________________

Preference __________________

A. Reason for this application

I am applying for lawful permanent residence for the following reason: (check the box that applies)

1. ☐ An immigrant visa number is immediately available to me because
   - ☐ A visa petition has already been approved for me (approval notice is attached)
   - ☐ A visa petition is being filed with this application
2. ☐ I entered as the fiance(e) of a U.S. citizen and married within 90 days (approval notice and marriage certificate are attached)
3. ☐ I am an asylee eligible for adjustment
4. ☐ Other: __________________

B. Information about you

1. **Name** (Family name in CAPS)   (First)   (Middle)

2. **Address** (Number and Street) .   (Apartment Number)

   (Town or City)   (State/Country)   (ZIP/Postal Code)

3. **Place of Birth** (Town or City)   (State/Country)

4. **Date of Birth** (Mo/Day/Yr)

5. **Sex**
   - ☐ Male
   - ☐ Female

6. **Marital Status**
   - ☐ Married   ☐ Single
   - ☐ Widowed   ☐ Divorced

7. **Social Security Number**

8. **Alien Registration Number** (if any)

9. **Country of Citizenship**

10. **Have you ever applied for permanent resident status in the U.S.?**
    ☐ Yes   ☐ No
    (If Yes, give the date and place of filing and final disposition)

11. **On what date did you last enter the U.S.?**

12. **Where did you last enter the U.S.?** (City and State)

13. **What means of travel did you use?** (Plane, car, etc.)

14. **Were you inspected by a U.S. immigration officer?**
    ☐ Yes   ☐ No

15. **In what status did you last enter the U.S.?**
    (Visitor, student, exchange alien, crewman, temporary worker, without inspection, etc.)

16. **Give your name EXACTLY as it appears on your Arrival/Departure Record (Form I-94).**

17. **Arrival/Departure Record (I-94) Number**

18. **Visa Number**

19. **At what Consulate was your nonimmigrant visa issued?**   Date (Mo/Day/Yr)

20. **Have you ever been married before?**   ☐ Yes   ☐ No
    If Yes.   (Names of prior husbands/wives)   (Country of citizenship)   (Date marriage ended)

21. **Has your husband/wife ever been married before?**   ☐ Yes   ☐ No
    If Yes.   (Names of prior husbands/wives)   (Country of citizenship)   (Date marriage ended)

INITIAL RECEIPT	RESUBMITTED	RELOCATED		COMPLETED		
		Rec'd	Sent	Approved	Denied	Returned

22. List your present husband/wife, all of your sons and daughters, all of your brothers and sisters (If you have none, write "N/A")

Name	Relationship	Place of Birth	Date of Birth	Country of Residence	Applying With You?
					☐ Yes ☐ No
					☐ Yes ☐ No
					☐ Yes ☐ No
					☐ Yes ☐ No
					☐ Yes ☐ No
					☐ Yes ☐ No
					☐ Yes ☐ No
					☐ Yes ☐ No
					☐ Yes ☐ No
					☐ Yes ☐ No

23. List your present and past membership in or affiliation with every organization, association, fund, foundation, party, club, society or similar group in the United States or in any other country or place, and your foreign military service (If this does not apply, write "N/A")

A ____ 19 _____ to 19 _____
B ____ 19 _____ to 19 _____
C ____ 19 _____ to 19 _____
D ____ 19 _____ to 19 _____
E ____ 19 _____ to 19 _____
F ____ 19 _____ to 19 _____
G ____ 19 _____ to 19 _____

24. Have you ever, in or outside the United States:

a) knowingly committed any crime for which you have not been arrested?　　　　☐ Yes　☐ No

b) been arrested, cited, charged, indicted, convicted, fined, or imprisoned for breaking or violating any law or ordinance, including traffic regulations?　　　　☐ Yes　☐ No

c) been the beneficiary of a pardon, amnesty, rehabilitation decree, other act of clemency or similar action?　　　　☐ Yes　☐ No

If you answered Yes to (a), (b), or (c) give the following information about each incident.

Date	Place (City)	(State/Country)	Nature of offense	Outcome of case, if any
1)				
2)				
3)				
4)				
5)				

25. Have you ever received public assistance from any source, including the U.S. Government or any state, county, city or municipality?

☐ Yes　☐ No　(If Yes, explain, including the name(s) and Social Security number(s) you used.)

26. Do any of the following relate to you? (Answer Yes or No to each)

A. Have you been treated for a mental disorder, drug addiction, or alcoholism?　　☐ Yes　☐ No

B. Have you engaged in, or do you intend to engage in, any commercialized sexual activity?　　☐ Yes　☐ No

C. Are you or have you at any time been an anarchist, or a member of or affiliated with any Communist or other totalitarian party, including any subdivision or affiliate?　　☐ Yes　☐ No

D. Have you advocated or taught, by personal utterance, by written or printed matter, or through affiliation with an organization.

1) opposition to organized government　　☐ Yes　☐ No

2) the overthrow of government by force or violence　　☐ Yes　☐ No

3) the assaulting or killing of government officials because of their official character　　☐ Yes　☐ No

4) the unlawful destruction of property　　☐ Yes　☐ No

5) sabotage　　☐ Yes　☐ No

6) the doctrines of world communism, or the establishment of a totalitarian dictatorship in the United States?　　☐ Yes　☐ No

E. Have you engaged or do you intend to engage in prejudicial activities or unlawful activities of a subversive nature?　　☐ Yes　☐ No

F. During the period beginning March 23, 1933, and ending May 8, 1945, did you order, incite, assist, or otherwise participate in persecuting any person because of race, religion, national origin, or political opinion, under the direction of, or in association with any of the following:

1) the Nazi government in Germany　　☐ Yes　☐ No

2) any government in any area occupied by the military forces of the Nazi government in Germany　　☐ Yes　☐ No

3) any government established with the assistance or cooperation of the Nazi government of Germany　　☐ Yes　☐ No

4) any government that was an ally of the Nazi government of Germany　　☐ Yes　☐ No

G. Have you been convicted of a violation of any law or regulation relating to narcotic drugs or marijuana, or have you been an illicit trafficker in narcotic drugs or marijuana?　　☐ Yes　☐ No

Form approved
OMB No. 43–R0514

REQUEST FOR DETERMINATION THAT PROSPECTIVE IMMIGRANT IS AN INVESTOR
in order to be relieved from labor certification requirement
of Section 212(a)(14) of the Immigration and Nationality Act

FILL IN WITH TYPEWRITER OR PRINT IN BLOCK LETTERS WITH BALLPOINT PEN. DO NOT LEAVE ANY QUESTION UNANSWERED. When appropriate insert "None" or "Not Applicable". If you need more space to answer fully any question on this form use a separate sheet of paper this size and identify each answer with the number of the corresponding question.

I hereby declare that I am seeking to become a lawful permanent resident of the United States for the purpose of engaging in an enterprise, and that I have invested, or am actively in the process of investing, in such enterprise capital totaling at least $40,000. On the basis of such investment, I request that the labor certification requirement of Section 212(a)(14) of the Immigration and Nationality Act be considered not applicable to me.

☐ I am submitting this request as part of my application to become a lawful permanent resident of the United States

☐ I am submitting this request as part of my application for an immigrant visa

1. Name *(Last in CAPS)* *(First)* *(Middle)* Alien registration number *(if any)*	**FOR GOVERNMENT USE ONLY** ☐ Approved ☐ Denied DATE OF ACTION DD DISTRICT

2. Other names used *(Married woman give maiden name)*

3. Place of Birth *(City or town)*   *(Country)*   4. Date of Birth *(Mo/Day/Yr)*

5. Present address *(Number and street)*   *(City or town)*   *(Province or State, Zip Code)*   *(Country)*

6. Name and location of enterprise

7. Names and immigration status of partners *(if applicable)*

8. Percentage of partnership or stock owned by applicant. List other owners and percentage of stock owned by them.

9. Nature of enterprise (Describe briefly; include total number of persons employed or to be employed in the enterprise and relationship, if any, to the applicant. Give name, home address, immigration status and relationship of at least one employee other than your spouse and children.)

10. Show source or potential source of investment funds.

11. Check one: ☐ I have made the investment   ☐ I am actively in the process of making the investment

12. The capital investment I made or am actively in the process of making consists of:

Cash $______________

Other $______________ (describe) ______________________

Other $______________ (describe) ______________________

TOTAL $______________

13. Describe briefly how you will engage in the enterprise, including the title of any job you will hold in it and the number of hours per week you will devote to the job.

Form I–526 (Rev. 12–22–79)N

RECEIVED	TRANS. IN	RET'D-TRANS. OUT	COMPLETED

14. EXPERIENCE—Employment or training you have had which qualify you to engage in the enterprise:

Name and address of employer or trainer

Name of Job	Date started *month year*	Date left *month year*	Kind of business

Describe in detail duties you performed, including use of tools, machines, or equipment, number of hours per week.

Name and address of employer or trainer

Name of Job	Date started *month year*	Date left *month year*	Kind of business

Describe in detail duties you performed, including use of tools, machines, or equipment, number of hours per week.

15. Describe any additional qualifications you possess for engaging in the enterprise.

16. List licenses (professional, journeyman, etc.) you have received.

17. I have attached the following documentary evidence (check each box applicable).

☐ Financial statements, such as balance sheet, or profit and loss statement
☐ License or other official authorization to engage in business in U.S.

☐ Corporate charter or partnership agreement   ☐ School records, certificates or diplomas   ☐ Employment letters
☐ Bank statement showing bank balance   ☐ Lease or deed to premises   ☐ Cancelled checks
☐ Licenses received outside the U.S.   ☐ Business contracts   ☐ Receipts
☐ Other (describe briefly)

18. If your native alphabet is in other than Roman Letters, write your name in your native alphabet below.

Signature of applicant

Date of signature

19. (Signature of person preparing form, if other than applicant) I declare that this document was prepared by me at the request of the applicant and is based on all information on which I have any knowledge.

Address of person preparing form, if other than applicant

Date:

Occupation:

REQUEST FOR ASYLUM IN THE UNITED STATES

INS Office:

Date:

1. Family Name   First   Middle Name

2. A number (if any or known)

All other names used at any time (include maiden name if married)

3. Sex
☐ Male
☐ Female

4. Marital status
☐ Single   ☐ Divorced
☐ Married   ☐ Widowed

I was born: (Month)   (Day)   (Year)   in (Town or City)   (State or Province)   (Country)

Nationality — at birth   At present   Other nationalities

5. If stateless, how did you become stateless?

6. Ethnic group

7. Religion

8. Languages spoken

9. Address in United States (In care of, C/O, if appropriate)
(Number and street)   (Apt. No.)   (City or town)   (State)   (Zip Code)

10. Telephone number (include area code)

11. Address abroad prior to coming to the United States
(Number and street)   (City)   (Province)   (Country)

12. My last arrival in the U.S. occurred on: (Mo/Day/Yr)

As a ☐ Visitor ☐ Student ☐ Stowaway ☐ Crewman
☐ Other (Specify)

At the port of (City/State)

Means of arrival (Name of vessel or airline and flight number, etc.)

I ☐ was ☐ was not inspected

Date authorized stay expires (Mo/Day/Yr)

13. My nonimmigrant visa number is _______________, it was issued by the U.S. Consul on__________
(If none, state "none")   (Mo/Day/Yr)
at________________________________
(City, County)

14. Name and location of schools attended	Type of school	From Mo/Yr	To Mo/Yr	Highest grade completed	Title of degree or certification

15. What specific skills do you have?

16. Social Security No. (if any)

17. Name of husband or wife (wife's maiden name)

18. My husband or wife resides ☐ with me ☐ apart from me (if apart, explain why)

Address (Apt. No.)   (No. and street)   (Town or city)   (Province or state)   (Country)

19. If in the U.S. is your spouse included in your request for asylum? ☐ Yes ☐ No (If not, explain why)

20. If in the U.S. is spouse making separate application for asylum? ☐ Yes ☐ No (If not, explain why)

21. If in the U.S. are children included in your request for asylum? ☐ Yes ☐ No (If not, explain why)

22. I have ——— sons or daughters as follows: (Complete all columns as to each son or daughter. If living with you state "with me" in last column; otherwise give city and state or foreign country of son's or daughter's residence).

Name	Sex	Place of birth	Date of birth	Now living at

23. Relatives in U.S. other than immediate family

Name	Address	Relationship	Immigration status

24. Other relatives who are refugees but outside the U.S.

Name	Relationship	Country where presently located

25. List all travel or identity documents such as national passport, refugee convention travel document or national identity card

Document type	Document number	Issuing country or authority	Date of issue	Date of expiration	Cost	Obtained by whom

26. Why did you obtain a U.S. visa?

27. If you did not apply for a U.S. visa, explain why not?

28. Date of departure from your country of nationality (Mo/Day/Yr)

29. Was exit permission required to leave your country? ☐ Yes ☐ No (If so, did you obtain exit permission ☐ Yes ☐ No (If not, explain why)

30. Are you entitled to return to country of issuance of your passport ☐ Yes ☐ No Travel document ☐ Yes ☐ No Or other document ☐ Yes ☐ No (If not, explain why)

31. What do you think would happen to you if you returned? (Explain)

32. When you left your home country, to what country did you intend to go?

33. Would you return to your home country? ☐ Yes ☐ No (Explain)

34. Have you or any member of your immediate family ever belonged to any organization in your home country? ☐ Yes ☐ No. (If yes, provide the following information relating to each organization: Name of organization, dates of membership or affiliation, purpose of the organization, what, if any, were your official duties or responsibilities, and are you still an active member. (If not, explain)

35. Have you taken any action that you believe will result in persecution in your home country? ☐ Yes ☐ No (If yes, explain)

36. Have you ever been ☐ detained ☐ interrogated ☐ convicted and sentenced ☐ imprisoned in any country? ☐ Yes ☐ No (If yes, specify for each instance: what occurred and the circumstances, dates, location, duration of the detention or imprisonment, reason for the detention or conviction, what formal charges were placed against you, reason for the release, names and addresses of persons who could verify these statements. Attach documents referring to these incidents, if any).

37. If you base your claim for asylum on current conditions in your country, do these conditions affect your freedom more than the rest of that country's population? ☐ Yes ☐ No (If yes, explain)

38. Have you, or any member of your immediate family, ever been mistreated by the authorities of your home country/country of nationality ☐ Yes ☐ No. If yes, was it mistreatment because of ☐ Race ☐ Religion ☐ Nationality ☐ Political opinion or ☐ Membership of a particular social group? Specify for each instance; what occurred and the circumstances, date, exact location, who took such action against you and what was his/her position in the government, reason why the incident occurred, names and addresses of people who witnessed these actions and who could verify these statements. Attach documents referring to these incidents.

39. After leaving your home country, have you traveled through (other than in transit) or resided in any other country before entering the U.S.? ☐ Yes ☐ No (If yes, identify each country, length of stay, purpose of stay, address, and reason for leaving, and whether you are entitled to return to that country for residence purposes.

40. Why did you continue traveling to the U.S.?

41. Did you apply for asylum in any other country? ☐ Yes—Give details ☐ No—Explain why not

42. Have you been recognized as a refugee by another country or by the United Nations High Commissioner for Refugees? ☐ Yes ☐ No (If yes, where and when)

43. Are you registered with a consulate or any other authority of your home country abroad? ☐ Yes—Give details ☐ No—Explain why not

44. Is there any additional information not covered by the above questions? (If yes, explain)

45. Under penalties of perjury, I declare that the above and all accompanying documents are true and correct to the best of my knowledge and belief.

_______________________________________   _______________________________________
(Signature of Applicant)   (Date)

_______________________________________   _______________________________________
(Interviewing Officer)   (Date of Interview)

ACTION BY ADJUDICATING OFFICER   ☐ GRANTED   ☐ DENIED

_______________________________________   _______________________________________
(Adjudicating Officer)   (Date)

Advisory opinion requested ☐   _______________________________________
                                                                   (Date)

114

U.S. Department of Justice
Immigration and Naturalization Service

Petition to Classify Orphan as an Immidiate Relative [Section 101 (b)(1)(F) of the Immigration and Nationality Act, as amended.]

Please do not write in this block.

TO THE SECRETARY OF STATE;

The petition was filed by:

☐ Married petitioner ☐ Unmarried petitioner

The petition is approved for orphan:

☐ Adopted abroad ☐ Coming to U.S. for adoption. Preadoption requirements have been met.

Remarks:

Fee Stamp

File number

DATE OF ACTION

DD

DISTRICT

Please type or print legibly in ink. Use a separate petition for each child.

Petition is being made to classify the named orphan as an immediate relative.

BLOCK I - Information About Prospective Petitioner

1. My name is: (Last) (First) (Middle)

2. Other names used (including maiden name if appropriate):

3. I reside in the U.S. at: (C/O if appropriate) (Apt. No.)

(Number and street) (Town or city) (State) (ZIP Code)

4. Address abroad (if any): (Number and street) (Apt. No.)

(Town or city) (Province) (Country)

5. I was born on: (Month) (Day) (Year)

In: (Town or City) (State or Province) (Country)

6. My phone number is: (Include Area Code)

7. My marital status is:

☐ Married
☐ Widowed
☐ Divorced
☐ Single
   ☐ I have never been married.
   ☐ I have been previously married _______ time(s).

8. If you are now married, give the following information:

Date and place of present marriage

Name of present spouse (include maiden name of wife)

Date of birth of spouse Place of birth of spouse

Number of prior marriages of spouse

My spouse resides ☐ With me ☐ Apart from me
(provide address below)

(Apt. No.) (No. and street) (City) (State) (Country)

9. I am a citizen of the United States through:

☐ Birth ☐ Parents ☐ Naturalization ☐ Marriage

If acquired through naturalization, give name under which naturalized, number of naturalization certificate, and date and place of naturalization:

If not, submit evidence of citizenship. See Instruction 2.a(2).

If acquired through parentage or marriage, have you obtained a certificate in your own name based on that acquisition?

☐ No ☐ Yes

Have you or any person through whom you claimed citizenship ever lost United States citizenship?

☐ No ☐ Yes (If yes, attach detailed explanation.)

Continue on reverse.

Received	Trans. In	Ret'd Trans. Out	Completed

Form I-600 (Rev. 4/11/91) Y

<table>
<tr><td colspan="2">

BLOCK II - Information About Orphan Beneficiary

</td></tr>
<tr><td>

10. Name at birth   (First)   (Middle)   (Last)

11. Name at present   (First)   (Middle)   (Last)

12. Any other names by which orphan is or was known.

13. Sex   ☐ Male   14. Date of birth (Month/Day/Year)   ☐ Female

15. Place of birth   (City)   (State or Province)   (Country)

16. The beneficiary is an orphan because (check one):
   ☐ He/she has no parents
   ☐ He/she has only one parent who is the sole or surviving parent.

17. If the orphan has only one parent, answer the following:
   a. State what has become of the other parent:

   b. Is the remaining parent capable of providing for the orphan's support?   ☐ Yes   ☐ No

   c. Has the remaining parent, in writing, irrevocably released the orphan for emigration and adoption?   ☐ Yes   ☐ No

18. Has the orphan been adopted abroad by the petitioner and spouse jointly or the unmarried petitioner?   ☐ Yes   ☐ No
   If yes, did the petitioner and spouse or unmarried petitioner personally see and observe the child prior to or during the adoption proceedings?   ☐ Yes   ☐ No

   Date of adoption

   Place of adoption

19. If either answer in question 18 is "No", answer the following:
   a. Do petitioner and spouse jointly or does the unmarried petitioner intend to adopt the orphan in the United States?   ☐ Yes   ☐ No
   b. Have the preadoption requirements, if any, of the orphan's proposed state of residence been met?   ☐ Yes   ☐ No
   c. If b. is answered "No", will they be met later?   ☐ Yes   ☐ No

</td><td>

20. To petitioner's knowledge, does the orphan have any physical or mental affliction?   ☐ Yes   ☐ No
   If "Yes", name the affliction.

21. Who has legal custody of the child?

22. Name of child welfare agency, if any, assisting in this case:

23. Name of attorney abroad, if any, representing petitioner in this case.
   Address of above.

24. Address in the United States where orphan will reside.

25. Present address of orphan.

25. If orphan is residing in an institution, give full name of institution.

26. If orphan is not residing in an institution, give full name of person with whom orphan is residing.

27. Give any additional information necessary to locate orphan such as name of district, section, zone or locality in which orphan resides.

28. Location of American Consulate where application for visa will be made.
   (City in Foreign Country)   (Foreign Country)

</td></tr>
</table>

Certification of Prospective Petitioner	**Certification of Married Prospective Petitioner's Spouse**
I certify under penalty of perjury under the laws of the United States of America that the foregoing is true and correct and that I will care for an orphan/orphans properly if admitted to the United States.	I certify under penalty of perjury under the laws of the United States of America that the foregoing is true and correct and that my spouse and I will care for an orphan/orphans properly if admitted to the United States.
(Signature of Prospective Petitioner)	*(Signature of Prospective Petitioner)*
Executed on (Date)	Executed on (Date)

Signature of Person Preparing Form if Other Than Petitioner

I declare that this document was prepared by me at the request of the prospective petitioner and is based on all information of which I have any knowledge.

(Signature)

Address

Executed on (Date)

116

Petition to Classify Orphan as an Immediate Relative

1. **Eligibility.**

    a. *Child.* Under immigration law, an orphan is an alien child who has no parents because of the death or disappearance of, abandonment or desertion by, or separation or loss from both parents. An orphan is also a child who has only one parent who is not capable of taking care of the orphan and has, in writing, irrevocably released the orphan for emigration and adoption. A petition to classify an alien as an orphan may not be filed in behalf of a child in the United States unless that child is in parole status and has not been adopted in the United States. The petition must be filed before the child's sixteenth birthday.

    b. *Parent(s).* The petition may be filed by a married United States citizen and spouse or unmarried United States citizen at least twenty-five years of age. The spouse does not need to be a United States citizen.

    c. *Adoption abroad.* If the orphan was adopted abroad, it must be established that both the married petitioner and spouse or the unmarried petitioner personally saw and observed the child prior to or during the adoption proceedings. The adoption decree must show that a married petitioner and spouse adopted the child jointly or that an unmarried petitioner was at least twenty-five years of age at the time of the adoption.

    d. *Proxy adoption abroad.* If both the petitioner and spouse or the unmarried petitioner did not personally see and observe the child prior to or during the adoption proceedings abroad, the petitioner (and spouse, if married) must submit a statement indicating the petitioner's (and, if married, the spouse's) willingness and intent to readopt the child in the United States. If requested, the petitioner must submit a statement by an official of the state in which the child will reside that readoption is permissible in that state. In addition, evidence of compliance with the preadoption requirements, if any, of that state must be submitted.

    e. *Preadoption requirements.* If the orphan has not been adopted abroad, the petitioner and spouse or the unmarried petitioner must establish that the child will be adopted in the United States by the petitioner and spouse jointly or by the unmarried petitioner and that the preadoption requirement, if any, of the state of the orphan's proposed residence have been met.

2. **Filing petition for known child.** An orphan petition for a child who has been identified must be submitted on a completed Form I-600 with the certification of petitioner executed and the required fee. If the petitioner is married, the Form I-600 must also be signed by the petitioner's spouse. The petition must be accompanied by the following:

    a. Proof of United States citizenship of the petitioner.

        (1) If the petitioner is a citizen by reason of birth in the United States, submit the petitioner's birth certificate, or if birth certificate is unobtainable, a copy of petitioner's baptismal certificate under seal of the church, showing place of birth, (baptism must have occurred within 2 months after birth), or if birth or baptismal certificate cannot be obtained, affidavits of two United States citizens who have personal knowledge of petitioner's birth in the United States.

        (2) If the petitioner was born outside the United States and became a citizen through the naturalization or citizenship of a parent or husband and has not been issued a certificate of citizenship in his/her own name, submit evidence of the citizenship and marriage of the parent or husband, as well as termination of any prior marriages. Also, if petitioner claims citizenship through a parent, submit petitioner's birth certificate and a separate statement showing the date, place, and means of all his/her arrivals and departures into and out of the United States.

        (3) If petitioner's naturalization occurred within 90 days immediately preceding the filing of this petition, or if it occurred prior to September 27, 1906, the naturalization certificate must accompany the petition.

    An unexpired U.S. passport valid for five years may also be submitted.

    b. Proof of marriage of petitioner and spouse.
        The married petitioner should submit a certificate of the marriage and proof of termination of all prior marriages of himself/herself and spouse. In the case of an unmarried petitioner who was previously married, submit proof of termination of all prior marriages. NOTE: If any change occurs in the petitioner's marital status while the case is pending, the District Director should be notified immediately.

    c. Proof of age of orphan.
        Petitioner should submit certificate of orphan's birth if obtainable; if not obtainable, submit an explanation together with the best available evidence of birth.

    d. Death certificate(s) of the child's parent(s), if applicable.

    e. A certified copy of adoption decree together with certified translation, if the orphan has been lawfully adopted abroad.

    f. Evidence that the sole or surviving parent is incapable of providing for the orphan's care and has in writing irrevocably released the orphan for emigration and adoption, if the orphan has only one parent.

    g. Evidence that the orphan has been unconditionally abandoned to an orphanage, if the orphan has been placed in an orphanage by his/her parent or parents.

    h. Evidence that the preadoption requirements, if any, of the state of the orphan's proposed residence have been met, if the child is to be adopted in the United States. If it is not possible to submit this evidence upon initial filing of the petition under the laws of the state of proposed residence, it may be submitted later. The petition, however, will not be approved without it.

    i. A home study with a statement or attachment recommending or approving of the adoption or proposed adoption signed by an official of the responsible state agency in the state of the child's proposed residence or of an agency authorized by that state, or, in the case of a child adopted abroad, of an appropriate public or private adoption agency which is licensed in the United States. Both individuals and organizations may qualify as agencies. If the recommending agency is a licensed agency, the recommendation must set forth that it is licensed, the state in which it is licensed, its license number, if any, and the period of validity of its license. The research, including interviewing, however, and the preparation of the home study may be done by an individual or group in the United States or abroad satisfactory to the recommending agency. A responsible state agency or licensed agency can accept a home study made by an unlicensed or foreign agency and use that home study as a basis for a favorable recommendation. The home study must contain, but is not limited to, the following elements:

Form I-600 (Rev. 4/11/91) Y

(1) The financial ability of the adoptive or prospective parent or parents to read and educate the child.

(2) A detailed description of the living accommodations where the adoptive or prospective parent or parents currently reside.

(3) A detailed description of the living accommodations where the child will reside.

(4) A factual evaluation of the physical, mental, and moral capabilities of the adoptive or prospective parent or parents in relation to rearing and educating the child.

j. Fingerprints.
Completed fingerprint cards (Forms FD-258) must be submitted by both the married petitioner and spouse or by the unmarried petitioner. The cards are available at any office of the Immigration and Naturalization Service. The fingerprints may be recorded on Form FD-258 by Service employees, other law enforcement officers, Service outreach centers, charitable and voluntary agencies, and any other reputable persons or organizations.

3. **Filing petition for known child without full documentation on child or home study.** When a child has been identified but the documentary evidence relating to him/her or the home study is not yet available, an orphan petition may be filed without that evidence or home study. The evidence outlined in Instructions 2a, 2b, and 2j, however, must be submitted. If the necessary evidence relating to the child or the home study is not submitted within one year from the date of submission of the petition, the petition will be considered abandoned, and the fee will not be refunded. Any further proceeding will require the filing of a new petition.

4. **Submitting an application for advance processing of an orphan petition in behalf of a child who has not been identified.** A prospective petitioner may request advance processing when the child has not been identified or when the prospective petitioner and/or spouse are/is going abroad to locate or adopt a child. If unmarried, the prospective petitioner must be at least twenty-four years of age provided that he/she will be at least twenty-five at the time of the adoption and the completed petition in behalf of a child is filed. The request must be on Form I-600A, Application for Advance Processing of Orphan Petition, and must be accompanied by the evidence required by that form. After a child or children are located and/or identified, a separate Form I-600, Petition to Classify Orphan as an Immediate Relative, must be filed for each child. A new fee is not required if only one Form I-600 is filed, if it is filed within one year of completion of all advance processing in a case where there has been a favorable determination concerning the prospective petitioner's ability to care for a beneficiary orphan. Normally, Form I-600 should be submitted to the office of this Service where the advance processing application was filed. A prospective petitioner who is going abroad to adopt or locate a child in a country other than Austria, Germany, Greece, Italy, Korea, the Philippines, Hong Kong, Mexico, Singapore, Uruguay, or Thailand, however, should file Form I-600 at the American consulate or embassy having jurisdiction over the place where the child is residing or will be located unless the case is being retained at the stateside office. A prospective petitioner who is going aboard to adopt or locate a child in Austria, Germany, Greece, Italy, Korea, the Philippines, Singapore, Hong Kong, Mexico, Uruguay, or Thailand should file Form I-600 at the Service office having jurisdiction over the place where the child is residing or will be located unless the case is being retained at the stateside office. The case may be retained at the stateside office if the petitioner requests it and it appears that the case will be processed more quickly that way.

5. **Documents in General.** All supporting documents must be originals or official copies of the original records issued by and bearing the seals of the official custodians of the records. If return of the originals is desired and if copies are by law permitted to be made, photostatic or typewritten copies may be submitted. A photostatic copy unaccompanied by the original may be accepted if the copy bears a certification by an immigration or consular office that the copy was compared with the original and found to be identical. Any document in a foreign language must be accompanied by a translation in English. The translator must certify that he/she is competent to translate and that the translation is accurate. **Do not make a photostat of a certificate of naturalization or citizenship.**

Submission of petition. A petitioner residing in the United States should send the completed petition to the office of this Service having jurisdiction over his//her place of residence. A petitioner residing outside the United States should consult the nearest American consulate or embassy designated to act on the petition.

7. **Fee. Read instructions carefully.** A fee of one hundred forty dollars ($140) must be paid for filing this petition. It cannot be refunded regardless of the action taken on the petition. **Do not mail cash. All fees must be submitted in the exact amount.** Payment by check or money order must be drawn on a bank or other institution located in the United States and be payable in United States currency. If petitioner resides in Guam, check or money order must be payable to the "Treasurer, Guam". If petitioner resides in the Virgin Islands, check or money order must be payable to the "Commissioner of Finance of the Virgin Islands". All other petitioners must make the check or money order payable to the "Immigration and Naturalization Service". When a check is drawn on the account of a person other than the petitioner, the name of the petitioner must be entered on the face of the check. If petition is submitted from outside the United States, remittance may be made by bank international money order or foreign draft drawn on a financial institution in the United States and payable to the Immigration and Naturalization Service in United States currency. Personal checks are accepted subject to collectibility. An uncollectible check will render the petition and any document issued pursuant to it invalid. A charge of $5.00 will be imposed if a check in payment of a fee is not honored by the bank on which it is drawn. **When more than one petition is submitted by the same petitioner in behalf of orphans who are brothers and/or sisters, only one fee will be required.**

8. **Assistance.** Assistance may be obtained from a recognized social agency or from any public or private agency. The following recognized social agencies, which have offices in may of the principal cities of the United States, have agreed to furnish assistance:

> **American Branch of International Social Services, Inc.**
> 345 East 46th Street
> New York, New York 10017
>
> **Greek Archdiocese of North and South America**
> 10 East 79th Street
> New York, New York 10021
>
> **United HIAS Service, Inc.**
> 200 Park Avenue South
> New York, New York 10003
>
> **Catholic Committee for Refugees**
> **United States Catholic Conference**
> 201 Park Avenue South
> New York, New York 10003
>
> **Church World Service, Inc.**
> 475 Riverside Drive
> New York, New York 10027

9. **Penalties.** Willful false statements on this form or supporting documents can be punished by fine or imprisonment. U.S. Code, Title 18, Sec. 1001 (Formerly Sec. 80.)

10. **Authority.** 8 U.S.C 1154(a). Routine uses for disclosure under the Privacy Act of 1974 have been published in the Federal Register and are available upon request. The Immigration and Naturalization Service will use the information to determine immigrant eligibility. Submission of the information is voluntary, but failure to provide any or all of the information may result in denial of the petition.

11. **Reporting Burden.** Public reporting burden for this collection of information is estimated to average 30 minutes per response, including the time for reviewing instructions, searching existing data sources, gathering and maintaining the data needed, and completing and reviewing the collection of information. Send comments regarding this burden estimate or any other aspect of this collection of information, including suggestions for reducing this burden, to: U.S. Department of Justice, Immigration and Naturalization Service (Room 5304), Washington, D.C. 20536; and to the Office of Management and Budget, Paperwork Reduction Project, OMB No. 1115-0049, Washington, D.C. 20503.

*U.S.GPO:1993-301-164/92708

OMB No. 1115-0049
Application for Advance Processing
of Orphan Petition [8CFR 204.1(b)(3)]

Please do not write in this block.

It has been determined that the

☐ Married   ☐ Unmarried

prospective petitioner will furnish proper care to a beneficiary orphan if admitted to the United Sates.

There

☐ are   ☐ are not

preadoptive requirements in the state of the child's proposed residence.

The following is a description of the preadoption requirements, if any, of the state of the child's proposed residence:

The preadoption requirements, if any,

☐ have been met.   ☐ have not been met.

Fee Stamp

DATE OF FAVORABLE DETERMINATION

DD

DISTRICT

File number of petitioner, if applicable

Please type or print legibly in ink.

Application is made by the named prospective petitioner for advance processing of an orphan petition.

BLOCK I - Information About Prospective Petitioner

1. My name is: (Last)   (First)   (Middle)

2. Other names used (including maiden name if appropriate):

3. I reside in the U.S. at: (C/O if appropriate)   (Apt. No.)

(Number and street)   (Town or city)   (State)   (ZIP Code)

4. Address abroad (if any): (Number and street)   (Apt. No.)

(Town or city)   (Province)   (Country)

5. I was born on: (Month)   (Day)   (Year)

In: (Town or City)   (State or Province)   (Country)

6. My phone number is: (Include Area Code)

7. My marital status is:
   ☐ Married
   ☐ Widowed
   ☐ Divorced
   ☐ Single
      ☐ I have never been married.
      ☐ I have been previously married __________ time(s).

8. If you are now married, give the following information:

Date and place of present marriage

Name of present spouse (include maiden name of wife)

Date of birth of spouse   Place of birth of spouse

Number of prior marriages of spouse

My spouse resides ☐ With me   ☐ Apart from me
(provide address below)

(Apt. No.)   (No. and street)   (City)   (State)   (Country)

9. I am a citizen of the United States through:
   ☐ Birth   ☐ Parents   ☐ Naturalization   ☐ Marriage

If acquired through naturalization, give name under which naturalized, number of naturalization certificate, and date and place of naturalization:

If not, submit evidence of citizenship. See Instruction 2.a(2).

If acquired through parentage or marriage, have you obtained a certificate in your own name based on that acquisition?

☐ No   ☐ Yes

Have you or any person through whom you claimed citizenship ever lost United States citizenship?

☐ No   ☐ Yes (If yes, attach detailed explanation.)

Continue on reverse.

Received	Trans. In	Ret'd Trans. Out	Completed

Form I-600A (Rev. 4/11/91) Y

BLOCK II - General Information

10. Name and address of organization or individual assisting you in locating or identifying an orphan

(Name)

____

(Address)

11. Do you plan to travel abroad to locate or adopt a child?

☐ Yes   ☐ No

12. Does your spouse, if any, plan to travel abroad to locate or adopt a child?

☐ Yes   ☐ No

13. If the answer to question 11 or 12 is "yes", give the following information:

    a. Your date of intended departure _______________

    b. Your spouse's date of intended departure _______________

    c. City, province _______________

14.. Will the child come to the United States for adoption after compliance with the preadoption requirements, if any, of the state of proposed residence?

☐ Yes   ☐ No

15. If the answer to question 14 is "no", will the child be adopted abroad after having been personally seen and observed by you and your spouse, if married?

☐ Yes   ☐ No

16. Where do you wish to file your orphan petition?

The service office located at

____

The American Consulate or Embassy at

17. Do you plan to adopt more than one child?

☐ Yes   ☐ No

If "Yes", how many children do you plan to adopt?

Certification of Prospective Petitioner

I certify under penalty of perjury under the laws of the United States of America that the foregoing is true and correct and that I will care for an orphan/orphans properly if admitted to the United States.

(Signature of Prospective Petitioner)

Executed on (Date)

Certification of Married Prospective Petitioner's Spouse

I certify under penalty of perjury under the laws of the United States of America that the foregoing is true and correct and that my spouse and I will care for an orphan/orphans properly if admitted to the United States.

(Signature of Prospective Petitioner)

Executed on (Date)

Signature of Person Preparing Form if Other Than Petitioner

I declare that this document was prepared by me at the request of the prospective petitioner and is based on all information of which I have any knowledge.

(Signature)

Address

Executed on (Date)

Advanced processing is a precedure for completing the part of an orphan petition relating to the petitioner before an orphan is located so that there will be no unnecessary delays in processing the petition after an orphan is located.
USE THIS FORM ONLY IF YOU WISH TO ADOPT AN ORPHAN WHO HAS NOT YET BEEN LOCATED AND IDENTIFIED OR YOU AND OR YOUR SPOUSE, IF MARRIED, ARE/IS GOING ABROAD TO ADOPT OR LOCATE A CHILD.
This application is not a petition to classify orphan as an immediate relative (Form I-600).

1. **Eligibility**

   a. Eligibility for advance processing application (Form I-600A). An application for advance processing may be filed by a married United States citizen and spouse. The spouse does not need to be a United States citizen. It may also be filed by an unmarried United States citizen at least twenty-four years of age provided that he/she will be at least twenty-five at the time of the adoption and of filing an orphan petition in behalf of a child.

   b. Eligibility for Orphan Petition (Form I-600). In addition to the requirements concerning the citizenship and age of the petitioner described in Instruction 1a, when a child is located and identified, the following eligibility requirements will apply:

      (1) *Child.* Under immigration law, an orphan is an alien child who has no parents because of the death or disappearance of, abandonment or desertion by, or separation or loss from both parents. An orphan is also a child who has only one parent who is not capable of taking care of the orphan and has, in writing, irrevocably released the orphan for emigration and adoption. A petition to classify an alien as an orphan may not be filed in behalf of a child in the United States unless that child is in parole status and has not been adopted in the Untied States. The petition must be filed before the child's sixteenth birthday.

      (2) *Adoption abroad.* If the orphan was adopted abroad, it must be established that both the married petitioner and spouse or the unmarried petitioner personally saw and observed the child prior to or during the adoption proceedings. The adoption decree must show that a married petitioner and spouse adopted the child jointly or that an unmarried petitioner was at least twenty-five years of age at the time of the adoption.

      (3) *Proxy adoption abroad.* If both the petitioner and spouse or the unmarried petitioner did not personally see and observe the child prior to or during the adoption proceedings abroad, the petitioner (and spouse, if married) must submit a statement indicating the petitioner's (and, if married, the spouse's) willingness and intent to readopt the child in the United States. If requested, the petitioner must submit a statement by an official of the state in which the child will reside that readoption is permissible in that state. In addition, evidence of compliance with the preadoption requirements, if any, of that state must be submitted.

      (4) *Preadoption requirements.* If the orphan has not been adopted abroad, the petitioner and spouse or the unmarried petitioner must establish that the child will be adopted in the United States by the petitioner and spouse jointly or by the unmarried petitioner and that the preadoption requirement, if any, of the state of the orphan's proposed residence have been met.

2. **Filing advance processing application.** An advance processing application must be submitted on Form I-600A with the certification of prospective petitioner executed and the required fee. If the prospective petitioner is married, the Form I-600A must also be signed by the prospective petitioner's spouse. The application must be accompanied by:

   a. Proof of United States citizenship of the prospective petitioner.

      (1) If the petitioner is a citizen by reason of birth in the United States, submit the petitioner's birth certificate, or if birth certificate is unobtainable, a copy of petitioner's baptismal certificate under seal of the church, showing place of birth, (baptism must have occurred within 2 months after birth), or if birth or baptismal certificate cannot be obtained, affidavits of two United States citizens who have personal knowledge of petitioner's birth in the United States.

      (2) If the petitioner was born outside the United States and became a citizen through the naturalization or citizenship of a parent or husband and has not been issued a certificate of citizenship in his/her own name, submit evidence of the citizenship and marriage of the parent or husband, as well as termination of any prior marriages. Also, if petitioner claims citizenship through a parent, submit petitioner's birth certificate and a separate statement showing the date, place, and means of all his/her arrivals and departures into and out of the United States.

      (3) If petitioner's naturalization occurred within 90 days immediately preceding the filing of this petition, or if it occurred prior to September 27, 1906, the naturalization certificate must accompany the petition.

   An unexpired U.S. passport valid for five years may also be submitted.

   b. Proof of marriage of petitioner and spouse.
   The married petitioner should submit a certificate of the marriage and proof of termination of all prior marriages of himself/herself and spouse. In the case of an unmarried petitioner who was previously married, submit proof of termination of all prior marriages. NOTE: If any change occurs in the petitioner's marital status while the case is pending, the District Director should be notified immediately.

   c. A home study with a statement or attachment recommending or approving of the adoption or proposed adoption signed by an official of the responsible state agency in the state of the child's proposed residence or of an agency authorized by that state, or, in the case of a child adopted abroad, of an appropriate public or private adoption agency which is licensed in the United States. Both individuals and organizations may qualify as agencies. If the recommending agency is a licensed agency, the recommendation must set forth that it is licensed, the state in which it is licensed, its license number, if any, and the period of validity of its license. The research, including interviewing, however, and the preparation of the home study may be done by an individual or group in the United States or abroad satisfactory to the recommending agency. A responsible state agency or licensed agency can accept a home study made by an unlicensed or foreign agency and use that home study as a basis for a favorable recommendation. The home study must contain, but is not limited to, the following elements:

121

(1) The financial ability of the adoptive or prospective parent or parents to read and educate the child.

(2) A detailed description of the living accommodations where the adoptive or prospective parent or parents currently reside.

(3) A detailed description of the living accommodations where the child will reside.

(4) A factual evaluation of the physical, mental, and moral capabilities of the adoptive or prospective parent or parents in relation to rearing and educating the child.

d. Fingerprints.
Completed fingerprint cards (Forms FD-258) must be submitted by both the married petitioner and spouse or by the unmarried petitioner. The cards are available at any office of the Immigration and Naturalization Service. The fingerprints may be recorded on Form FD-258 by Service employees, other law enforcement officers, Service outreach centers, charitable and voluntary agencies, and any other reputable persons or organizations.

3. **Documents in General.** All supporting documents must be originals or official copies of the original records issued by and bearing the seals of the official custodians of the records. If return of the originals is desired and if copies are by law permitted to be made, photostatic or typewritten copies may be submitted. A photostatic copy unaccompanied by the original may be accepted if the copy bears a certification by an immigration or consular office that the copy was compared with the original and found to be identical. Any document in a foreign language must be accompanied by a translation in English. The translator must certify that he/she is competent to translate and that the translation is accurate. **Do not make a photostat of a certificate of naturalization or citizenship.**

4. **Submission of application.** A prospective petitioner residing in the United States should send the completed application to the office of this Service having jurisdiction over his//her place of residence. A prospective petitioner residing outside the United States should consult the nearest American consulate for the overseas or stateside office of this Service designated to act on the application.

5. **Fee. Read instructions carefully.** A fee of one hundred forty dollars ($140) must be paid for filing this petition. It cannot be refunded regardless of the action taken on the petition. **Do not mail cash. All fees must be submitted in the exact amount.** Payment by check or money order must be drawn on a bank or other institution located in the United States and be payable in United States currency. If petitioner resides in Guam, check or money order must be payable to the "Treasurer, Guam". If petitioner resides in the Virgin Islands, check or money order must be payable to the "Commissioner of Finance of the Virgin Islands". All other petitioners must make the check or money order payable to the "Immigration and Naturalization Service". When a check is drawn on the account of a person other than the petitioner, the name of the petitioner must be entered on the face of the check. If petition is submitted from outside the United States, remittance may be made by bank international money order or foreign draft drawn on a financial institution in the United States and payable to the Immigration and Naturalization Service in United States currency. Personal checks are accepted subject to collectibility. An uncollectible check will render the petition and any document issued pursuant to it invalid. A charge of $5.00 will be imposed if a check in payment of a fee is not honored by the bank on which it is drawn. **When more than one petition is submitted by the same petitioner in behalf of orphans who are brothers and/or sisters, only one fee will be required.**

6. **When Child/children located and/or identified.** A separate Form I-600, Petition to Classify Orphan as an Immediate Relative, must be filed for each child. A new fee is not required if only one Form I-600 is filed and it is filed within one year of completion of all advance processing in a case where there has been a favorable determination concerning the prospective petitioner's ability to care for a beneficiary orphan. Normally, Form I-600 should be submitted to the office of this Service where the advance processing application was filed. A prospective petitioner who is going abroad to adopt or locate a child in a country other than Austria, Germany, Greece, Italy, Korea, the Philippines, Hong Kong, Mexico, Singapore, Uruguay, or Thailand, however, should file Form I-600 at the American consulate or embassy having jurisdiction over the place where the child is residing or will be located unless the case is being retained at the stateside office. A prospective petitioner who is going abroad to adopt or locate a child in Austria, Germany, Greece, Italy, Korea, the Philippines, Hong Kong, Mexico, Singapore, Uruguay, or Thailand should file Form I-600 at the Service office having jurisdiction over the place where the child is residing or will be located unless the case is being retained at the stateside office. The case may be retained at the stateside office if the petitioner requests it and it appears that the case will be processed more quickly that way. Form I-600 must be accompanied by all the evidence required on the instruction sheet of that form except that the evidence required by and submitted with this form need not be furnished.

7. **Assistance.** Assistance may be obtained from a recognized social agency or from any public or private agency. The following recognized social agencies, which have offices in may of the principal cities of the United States, have agreed to furnish assistance:

> **American Branch of International Social Services, Inc.**
> 345 East 46th Street
> New York, New York 10017
>
> **Greek Archdiocese of North and South America**
> 10 East 79th Street
> New York, New York 10021
>
> **United HIAS Service, Inc.**
> 200 Park Avenue South
> New York, New York 10003
>
> **Catholic Committee for Refugees**
> **United States Catholic Conference**
> 201 Park Avenue South
> New York, New York 10003
>
> **Church World Service, Inc.**
> 475 Riverside Drive
> New York, New York 10027

8. **Penalties.** Willful false statements on this form or supporting documents can be punished by fine or imprisonment. U.S. Code, Title 18, Sec. 1001 (Formerly Sec. 80.)

9. **Authority.** 8 U.S.C 1154(a). Routine uses for disclosure under the Privacy Act of 1974 have been published in the Federal Register and are available upon request. The Immigration and Naturalization Service will use the information to determine immigrant eligibility. Submission of the information is voluntary, but failure to provide any of all of the information may result in denial of the petition.

10. **Reporting Burden.** Public reporting burden for this collection of information is estimated to average 30 minutes per response, including the time for reviewing instructions, searching existing data sources, gathering and maintaining the data needed, and completing and reviewing the collection of information. Send comments regarding this burden estimate or any other aspect of this collection of information, including suggestions for reducing this burden, to: U.S. Department of Justice, Immigration and Naturalization Service (Room 5304), Washington, D.C.20536; and to the Office of Management and Budget, Paperwork Reduction Project, OMB No. 1115-0049, Washington, D.C. 20503.

Purpose Of This Form.
This form is for a conditional resident who obtained such status through marriage to apply to remove the conditions on his or her residence.

Who May File.
If you were granted conditional resident status through marriage to a U.S. citizen or permanent resident, use this form to petition for the removal of those conditions. Your petition should be filed jointly by you and the spouse through whom you obtained conditional status if you are still married. However, you can apply for a waiver of this joint filing requirement on this form if:

- you entered into the marriage in good faith, but your spouse subsequently died;
- you entered into the marriage in good faith, but the marriage was later terminated due to divorce or annulment;
- you entered nto the marriage in good faith, and remain married, but have been battered or subjected to extreme mental cruelty by your U.S. citizen or permanent resident spouse; or
- the termination of your status, and deportation, would result in extreme hardship.

You may include your conditional resident children in your petition, or they can file separately.

General Filing Instructions.
Please answer all questions by typing or clearly printing in black ink. Indicate that an item is not applicable with "N/A". If an answer is "none," write "none". If you need extra space to answer any item, attach a sheet of paper with your name and your alien registration number (A#), and indicate the number of the item to which the answer refers. You must file your petition with the required Initial Evidence. Your petition must be properly signed and accompanied by the correct fee. If you are under 14 years of age, your parent or guardian may sign the petition in your behalf.

Translations. Any foreign language document must be accompanied by a full English translation which the translator has certified as complete and correct, and by the translator's certification that he or she is competent to translate from the foreign language into English.

Copies. If these instructions state that a copy of a document may be filed with this petition, and you choose to send us the original, we may keep that original for our records.

Initial Evidence.
Alien Registration Card. You must file your petition with a copy of your alien registration card, and with a copy of the alien registration card of any of your conditional resident children you are including in your petition.

Evidence of the relationship. Submit copies of documents indicating that the marriage upon which you were granted conditional status was entered into in "good faith", and was not for the purpose of circumventing immigration laws. You should submit copies of as many documents as you wish to establish this fact and to demonstrate the circumstances of the relationship from the date of the marriage to date, and to demonstrate any circumstances surrounding the end of the relationship, if it has ended. The documents should cover as much of the period since your marriage as possible. Examples of such documents are:

- Birth certificate(s) of child(ren) born to the marriage.
- Lease or mortgage contracts showing joint occupancy and/ or ownership of your communal residence.
- Financial records showing joint ownership of assets and joint responsibility for liabilities, such as joint savings and checking accounts, joint federal and state tax returns, insurance policies which show the other as the beneficiary, joint utility bills, joint installment or other loans.
- Other documents you consider relevant to establish that your marriage was not entered into in order to evade the immigration laws of the United States.

- Affidavits sworn to or affirmed by at least 2 people who have known both of you since your conditional residence was granted and have personal knowledge of your marriage and relationship. (Such persons may be required to testify before an immigration officer as to the information contained in the affidavit.) The original affidavit must be submitted, and it must also contain the following information regarding the person making the affidavit: his or her full name and address; date and place of birth; relationship to you or your spouse, if any; and full information and complete details explaining how the person acquired his or her knowledge. Affidavits must be supported by other types of evidence listed above.

If you are filing to waive the joint filing requirement due to the death of your spouse, also submit a copy of the death certificate with your petition.

If you are filing to waive the joint filing requirement because your marriage has been terminated, also submit a copy of the divorce decree or other document terminating or annulling the marriage with your petition.

If you are filing to waive the joint filing requirement because you and/or your conditional resident child were battered or subjected to extreme mental cruelty, also file your petition with the following.

- Evidence of the physical abuse, such as copies of reports or official records issued by police, judges, medical personnel, school officials, and representatives of social service agencies, and original affidavits as described under *Evidence of the Relationship*; or
- Evidence of the extreme mental cruelty, and an original evaluation by a professional recognized by the Service as an expert in the field. These experts include clinical social workers, psychologists and psychiatrists. A clinical social worker who is not licensed only because the State in which he or she practices does not provide for licensing is considered a licensed professional recognized by the Service if he or she is included by the National Association of Social Workers or is certified by the American Board of Examiners in Clinical Social Work. Each evaluation must contain the professional's full name, professional address and license number. It must also identify the licensing, certifying or registering authority.
- A copy of your divorce decree if your marriage was terminated by divorce on grounds of physical abuse or mental cruelty.

If you are filing for a waiver of the joint filing requirement because the termination of your status, and deportation would result in "extreme hardship", you must also file your petition with evidence your deportation would result in hardship significantly greater than the hardship encountered by other aliens who are deported from this country after extended stays. The evidence must relate only to those factors which arose since you became a conditional resident.

If you are a child filing separately from your parent, also file your petition with a full explanation as to why you are filing separately, along with copies of any supporting documentation.

When To File.
Filing jointly. If you are filing this petition jointly with your spouse, you must file it during the 90 days immediately before the second anniversary of the date you were accorded conditional resident status. This is the date your conditional residence expires. However, if you and your spouse are outside the United States on orders of the U.S. Government during the period in which the petition must be filed, you may file it within 90 days of your return to the U.S.

Filing with a request that the joint filing requirement be waived. You may file this petition at any time after you are granted conditional resident status and before you are deported.

Effect Of Not Filing. If this petition is not filed, you will automatically lose your permanent resident status as of the second anniversary of the date on which you were granted this status. You will then become deportable from the United States. If your failure to file was through no fault of your own, you may file your petition late with a written explanation and request that INS excuse the late filing. Failure to file before the expiration date may be excused if you demonstrate when you file the application that the delay was due to extraordinary circumstances beyond your control and that the length of the delay was reasonable.

Effect of Filing.
Filing this petition extends your conditional residence for six months. You will receive a filing receipt which you should carry with your alien registration card (Form I-551). If you travel outside the U.S. during this period, you may present your card and the filing receipt to be readmitted.

Where To File.
If you live in Connecticut, Delaware, District of Columbia, Maine, Maryland, Massachusetts, New Hampshire, New Jersey, New York, Pennsylvania, Puerto Rico, Rhode Island, Vermont, Virgin Islands, Virginia, or West Virginia, mail your petition to: USINS Eastern Service Center, 75 Lower Welden Street, St. Albans, VT 05479-0001.

If you live in Alabama, Arkansas, Florida, Georgia, Kentucky, Louisiana, Mississippi, New Mexico, North Carolina, Oklahoma, South Carolina, Tennessee, or Texas, mail your petition to: USINS Southern Service Center, P.O. Box 152122, Dept. A, Irving, TX 75015-2122.

If you live in Arizona, California, Guam, Hawaii, or Nevada, mail your petition to: USINS Western Service Center, P.O. Box 30111, Laguna Niguel, CA 92607-0111.

If you live in elsewhere in the U.S., mail your petition to: USINS Northern Service Center, 100 Centennial Mall North, Room B-26, Lincoln, NE 68508.

Fee.
The fee for this petition is $75.00. The fee must be submitted in the exact amount. It cannot be refunded. **DO NOT MAIL CASH.**

All checks and money orders must be drawn on a bank or other institution located in the United States and must be payable in United States currency. The check or money order should be made payable to the Immigration and Naturalization Service, except that:
- If you live in Guam, and are filing this petition in Guam, make your check or money order payable to the "Treasurer, Guam".
- If you are living in the Virgin Islands, and are filing this application in the Virgin Islands, make your check or money order payable to the "Commissioner of Finance of the Virgin Islands".

Checks are accepted subject to collection. An uncollected check will render the application and any document issued invalid. A charge of $5.00 will be imposed if a check in payment of a fee is not honored by the bank on which it is drawn.

Processing Information.
Acceptance. Any petition that is not signed, or is not accompanied by the correct fee, will be rejected with a notice that the petition is deficient. You may correct the deficiency and resubmit the petition. A petition is not considered properly filed until accepted by the Service.

Initial processing. Once a petition has been accepted, it will be checked for completeness, including submission of the required initial evidence. If you do not completely fill out the form, or file if without required initial evidence, you will not establish a basis for eligibility, and we may deny your petition.

Requests for more information or Interview. We may request more information or evidence, or we may request that you appear at an INS office for an interview. We may also request that you submit the originals of any copy. We will return these originals when they are no longer required.

Decision. You will be advised in writing of the decision on your petition.

Penalties.
If you knowingly and willfully falsify or conceal a material fact or submit a false document with this request, we will deny the benefit you are filing for, and may deny any other immigration benefit. In addition, you will face severe penalties provided by law, and may be subject to criminal prosecution.

Privacy Act Notice.
We ask for the information on this form, and associated evidence, to determine if you have established eligibility for the immigration benefit you are filing for. Our legal right to ask for this information is in 8 USC 1184, 1255 and 1258. Failure to provide this information, and any requested evidence, may delay a final decision or result in denial of your request.

All the information provided on this form, including addresses, are protected by the Privacy Act and the Freedom of Information Act. This information will not be released in any form whatsoever to a third party, other than another government agency, who requests it without a court order, or without your written consent, or, in the case of a child, the written consent of the parent or legal guardian who filed the form on the child's behalf.

Paperwork Reduction Act Notice.
We try to create forms and instructions that are accurate, can be easily understood, and which impose the least possible burden on you to provide us with information. Often this is difficult because some immigration laws are very complex. The estimated average time to complete and file this application is as follows: (1) 15 minutes to learn about the law and form; (2) 15 minutes to complete the form; and (3) 50 minutes to assemble and file the petition; for a total estimated average of 1 hour and 20 minutes per petition. If you have comments regarding the accuracy of this estimate, or suggestions for making this form simpler, you can write to both the Immigration and Naturalization Service, 425 I Street, N.W., Room 5304, Washington, D.C. 20536; and the Office of Management and Budget, Paperwork Reduction Project, OMB No. 1115-0145 Washington, D.C. 20503.

Form I-751 (Rev. 12-4-91)

START HERE - Please Type or Print

Part 1. Information about you.

Family Name	Given Name	Middle Initial

Address - C/O:

Street Number and Name		Apt. #
City	State or Province	
Country	ZIP/Postal Code	

Date of Birth (month/day/year)	Country of Birth
Social Security #	A #

Conditional residence expires on (month/day/year)

Mailing address if different from residence in C/O:

Street Number and Name		Apt #
City	State or Province	
Country	ZIP/Postal Code	

FOR INS USE ONLY

Returned	Receipt

Resubmitted

Reloc Sent

Reloc Rec'd

☐ Applicant Interviewed

Remarks

Part 2. Basis for petition *(check one).*

a. ☐ My conditional residence is based on my marriage to a U.S. citizen or permanent resident, and we are filing this petition together.

b. ☐ I am a child who entered as a conditional permanent resident and I am unable to be included in a Joint Petition to Remove the Conditional Basis of Alien's Permanent Residence (Form I-751) filed by my parent(s).

My conditional residence is based on my marriage to a U.S. citizen or permanent resident, but I am unable to file a joint petition and I request a waiver because: (check one)

c. ☐ My spouse is deceased.

d. ☐ I entered into the marriage in good faith, but the marriage was terminated though divorce/annulment.

e. ☐ I am a conditional resident spouse who entered in to the marriage in good faith, or I am a conditional resident child, who has been battered or subjected to extreme mental cruelty by my citizen or permanent resident spouse or parent.

f. ☐ The termination of my status and deportation from the United States would result in an extreme hardship.

Action

Part 3. Additional information about you.

Other names used *(including maiden name)*:	Telephone #
Date of Marriage	Place of Marriage

If your spouse is deceased, give the date of death (month/day/year)

Are you in deportation or exclusion proceedings? ☐ Yes ☐ No

Was a fee paid to anyone other than an attorney in connection with this petition? ☐ Yes ☐ No

To Be Completed by Attorney or Representative, if any

☐ Fill in box if G-28 is attached to represent the applicant

VOLAG #

ATTY State License #

Form I-751 (Rev. 12-4-91)   *Continued on back.*

Part 3. Additional Information about you. (con't)

Since becoming a conditional resident, have you ever been arrested, cited, charged, indicted, convicted, fined or imprisoned for breaking or violating any law or ordinance (excluding traffic regulations), or committed any crime for which you were not arrested?   ☐ Yes ☐ No

If you are married, is this a different marriage than the one through which conditional residence status was obtained?   ☐ Yes ☐ No

Have you resided at any other address since you became a permanent resident?   ☐ Yes ☐ No *(If yes, attach a list of all addresses and dates.)*

Is your spouse currently serving employed by the U. S. government and serving outside the U.S.?   ☐ Yes ☐ No

Part 4. Information about the spouse or parent through whom you gained your conditional residence.

Family Name	Given Name	Middle Initial	Phone Number ( )

Address

Date of Birth (month/day/year)	Social Security #	A#

Part 5. Information about your children. *List __all__ your children.   Attach another sheet if necessary*

	Name	Date of Birth (month/day/year)	If in U.S., give A#, current immigration status and U.S. Address	Living with you?
1				☐ Yes ☐ No
2				☐ Yes ☐ No
3				☐ Yes ☐ No
4				☐ Yes ☐ No

Part 6. Complete if you are requesting a waiver of the joint filing petition requirement based on extreme mental cruelty.

Evaluator's ID Number: State: ☐☐ Number: ☐☐☐☐☐☐☐	Expires on (month/day/year)	Occupation

Last Name	First Name	Address

Part 7. Signature. *Read the information on penalties in the instructions before completing this section. If you checked block "a" in Part 2 your spouse must also sign below.*

I certify, under penalty of perjury under the laws of the United States of America, that this petition, and the evidence submitted with it, is all true and correct. If conditional residence was based on a marriage, I further certify that the marriage was entered into in accordance with the laws of the place where the marriage took place, and was not for the purpose of procuring an immigration benefit. I also authorize the release of any information from my records which the Immigration and Naturalization Service needs to determine eligibility for the benefit being sought.

Signature	Print Name	Date
Signature of Spouse	Print Name	Date

Please note: If you do not completely fill out this form, or fail to submit any required documents listed in the instructions, then you cannot be found eligible for the requested benefit, and this petition may be denied.

Part 8. Signature of person preparing form if other than above.

I declare that I prepared this petition at the request of the above person and it is based on all information of which I have knowledge.

Signature	Print Name	Date

Firm Name and Address

Application for Employment Authorization

How to File:

A separate application must be filed by each applicant. Applications must be typewritten or clearly printed in ink and completed in full. If extra space is needed to answer any item, attach a continuation sheet and indicate your name, A-number (if any) and the item number.

Note: It is recommended that you retain a complete copy of your application for your records.

Who should file this application?

Certain aliens temporarily in the United States are eligible for employment authorization. Please refer to the ELIGIBILITY SECTION of this application which is found on page three. Carefully review the classes of aliens described in Group A and Group C to determine if you are eligible to apply.

This application should not be filed by lawful permanent resident aliens or by lawful temporary resident aliens.

What is the fee?

Applicants must pay a fee of $60.00 to file this form <u>unless</u> otherwise noted on the reverse of the form. Please refer to page 3. If required, the fee will not be refunded. Pay by cash, check, or money order in the exact amount. All checks and money orders must be payable in U.S. currency in the United States. Make check or money order payable to "Immigration and Naturalization Service." However, if you live in Guam make it payable to "Treasurer, Guam," or if you live in the U.S. Virgin Islands make it payable to "Commissioner of Finance of the Virgin Islands." If the check is not honored the INS will charge you $5.00.

Where should you file this application?

Applications must be filed with the nearest Immigration and Naturalization Service (INS) office that processes employment authorization applications which has jurisdiction over your place of residence. You must appear in person to receive an employment authorization document. **Please bring your INS Form I-94 and any document issued to you by the INS granting you previous employment authorization.**

What is our authority for collecting this information?

The authority to require you to file Form I-765, Application for Employment Authorization, is contained in the "Immigration Reform and Control Act of 1986." This information is necessary to determine whether you are eligible for employment authorization and for the preparation of your Employment Authorization Document if you are found eligible. Failure to provide all information as requested may result in the denial or rejection of this application.

The information you provide may also be disclosed to other federal, state, local and foreign law enforcement and regulatory agencies during the course of the investigation required by this Service.

Basic Criteria to Establish Economic Necessity:

Title 45 - Public Welfare, Poverty Guidelines, 45 CFR 1060.2 may be used as the basic criteria to establish eligibility for employment authorization when the applicant's economic necessity is identified as a factor. If you are an applicant who must show economic necessity, you should include a statement listing all of your assets, income, and expenses as evidence of your economic need to work.

Note: Not all applicants are required to establish economic necessity. Carefully review the ELIGIBILITY SECTION of the application. Only aliens who are filing for employment authorization under Group C, items (c)(3) (i), (c)(13), (c)(14) and (c) (18) are required to furnish information on economic need. This information must be furnished on attached sheet(s) and submitted with this application.

What are the penalties for submitting false information?

Title 18, United States Code, Section 1001 states that whoever willfully and knowingly falsifies a material fact, makes a false statement, or makes use of a false document will be fined up to $10,000 or imprisoned up to five years, or both.

Title 18, United States Code, Section 1546(a) states that whoever makes any false statement with respect to a material fact in any document required by the immigration laws or regulations, or presents an application containing any false statement shall be fined or imprisoned or both.

Please Complete Both Sides of Form.

Do Not Write In This Block   **Please Complete Both Sides of Form**

Remarks	Action Stamp	Fee Stamp
A#		

Applicant is filing under 274a.12 ______

☐ Application Approved. Employment Authorized / Extended (Circle One) __________________ (Date).
    until __________________ (Date).

    Subject to the following conditions: __________________
☐ Application Denied.
    ☐ Failed to establish eligibility under 8 CFR 274a.12 (a) or (c).
    ☐ Failed to establish economic necessity as required in 8 CFR 274a.12(c) (13) (14) (18) and 8 CFR 214.2(f)

I am applying for: ☐ Permission to accept employment
               ☐ Replacement (of lost employment authorization document).
               ☐ Extension of my permission to accept employment (attach previous employment authorization document).

1. Name (Family Name in CAPS)   (First)   (Middle)

2. Other Names Used (Include Maiden Name)

3. Address in the United States (Number and Street)   (Apt. Number)

    (Town or City)   (State/Country)   (ZIP Code)

4. Country of Citizenship/Nationality

5. Place of Birth (Town or City) (State/Province) (Country)

6. Date of Birth (Month/Day/Year)   7. Sex   ☐ Male ☐ Female

8. Marital Status   ☐ Married   ☐ Single
             ☐ Widowed   ☐ Divorced

9. Social Security Number (Include all Numbers you have ever used)

10. Alien Registration Number (A-Number) or I-94 Number (if any)

11. Have you ever before applied for employment authorization from INS?
    ☐ Yes (If yes, complete below)   ☐ No
    Which INS Office?   Date(s)

    Results (Granted or Denied - attach all documentation)

12. Date of Last Entry into the U.S. (Month/Day/Year)

13. Place of Last Entry into the U.S.

14. Manner of Last Entry (Visitor, Student, etc.)

15. Current Immigration Status (Visitor, Student, etc.)

16. Go to the Eligibility Section on the reverse of this form and check the box which applies to you. In the space below, place the letter and number of the box you selected from the reverse side:

Eligibility under 8 CFR 274a.12

(   ) (   ) (   )

Complete the reverse of this form before signature.

Your Certification: I certify, under penalty of perjury under the laws of the United States of America, that the foregoing is true and correct. Furthermore, I authorize the release of any information which the Immigration and Naturalization Service needs to determine eligibility for the benefit I am seeking. I have read the reverse of this form and have checked the appropriate block, which is identified in item #16, above.

Signature   Telephone Number   Date

Signature of Person Preparing Form if Other Than Above: I declare that this document was prepared by me at the request of the applicant and is based on all information of which I have any knowledge.

Print Name   Address   Signature   Date

Initial Receipt	Resubmitted	Relocated		Completed		
		Rec'd	Sent	Approved	Denied	Returned

128

Form I-765 (Rev. 04/11/91) Y Page 2

Eligibility

GROUP A

The current immigration laws and regulations permit certain classes of aliens to work in the United States. If you are an alien described below, you do not need to request that employment authorization be granted to you, but you do need to request a document to show that you are able to work in the United States. For aliens in classes (a) (3) through (a) (11), **NO FEE** will be required for the original card or for extension cards. A **FEE** will be required if a replacement employment authorization document is needed. A **FEE IS REQUIRED** for aliens in item (a) (12) who are over the age of 14 years and under the age of 65 years.

Place an X in the box next to the number which applies to you.

☐   (a) (3) - I have been admitted to the United States as a refugee.

☐   (a) (4) - I have been paroled into the United States as a refugee.

☐   (a) (5) - My application for asylum has been granted.

☐   (a) (6) - I am the fiancé(e) of a United States citizen and I have K-1 nonimmigrant status; OR I am the dependent of a fiancé(e) of a United States citizen and I have K-2 nonimmigrant status.

☐   (a) (7) - I have N-8 or N-9 nonimmigrant status in the United States.

☐   (a) (8) - I am a citizen of the Federated States of Micronesia or of the Marshall Islands.

☐   (a) (10) - I have been granted withholding of deportation.

☐   (a) (11) - I have been granted extended voluntary departure by the Attorney General.

☐   (a) (12) - I am an alien who has been registered for Temporary Protected Status (TPS) and I want an employment authorization document. **FEE REQUIRED.**

GROUP C

The immigration law and regulations allow certain aliens to apply for employment authorization. If you are an alien described in one of the classes below you may request employment authorization from the INS and, if granted, you will receive an employment authorization document. The instruction **FEE REQUIRED** printed below refers to your initial document, replacement, and extension.

Place an X in the box next to the number which applies to you.

☐   (c) (1) - I am the dependent of a foreign government official (A-1 or A-2). I have attached certification from the Department of State recommending employment. **NO FEE.**

☐   (c) (2) - I am the dependent of an employee of the Coordination Council of North American Affairs and I have E-1 nonimmigrant status. I have attached certification of my status from the American Institute of Taiwan. **FEE REQUIRED.**

☐   (c) (3) (i) - I am a foreign student (F-1). I have attached certification from the designated school official recommending employment for economic necessity. I have also attached my INS Form I-20 ID copy. **FEE REQUIRED.**

☐   (c) (3) (ii) - I am a foreign student (F-1). I have attached certification from the designated school official recommending employment for practical training. I have also attached my INS Form I-20 ID copy. **FEE REQUIRED.**

☐   (c) (3) (iii) - I am a foreign student (F-1). I have attached certification from my designated school official and I have been offered employment under the sponsorship of an international organization within the meaning of the International Organization Immunities Act. I have certification from this sponsor and I have also attached my INS Form I-20 ID copy. **FEE REQUIRED**

☐   (c) (4) - I am the dependent of an officer or employee of an international organization (G-1 or G-4). I have attached certification from the Department of State recommending employment. **NO FEE.**

☐   (c) (5) - I am the dependent of an exchange visitor and I have J-2 nonimmigrant status. **FEE REQUIRED.**

☐   (c) (6) - I am a vocational foreign student (M-1). I have attached certification from the designated school official recommending employment for practical training. I have also attached my INS Form I-20 ID Copy. **FEE REQUIRED.**

☐   (c) (7) - I am the dependent of an individual classified as NATO-1 through NATO-7. **FEE REQUIRED.**

☐   (c) (8) - I have filed a non-frivolous application for asylum in the United States and the application is pending. **FEE REQUIRED FOR REPLACEMENT ONLY.**

☐   (c) (9) - I have filed an application for adjustment of status to lawful permanent resident status and the application is pending. **FEE REQUIRED.**

☐   (c) (10) - I have filed an application for suspension of deportation and the application is still pending. **FEE REQUIRED.**

☐   (c) (11) - I have been paroled into the United States for emergent reasons or for reasons in the public interest. **FEE REQUIRED.**

☐   (c) (12) - I am a deportable alien and I have been granted voluntary departure either prior to or after my hearing before the immigration judge. **FEE REQUIRED.**

☐   (c) (13) - I have been placed in exclusion or deportation proceedings. I have not received a final order of deportation or exclusion and I have not been detained. **I understand that I must show economic necessity and I will refer to the instructions concerning "Basic Criteria to Establish Economic Necessity."** **FEE REQUIRED.**

☐   (c) (14) - I have been granted deferred action by INS as an act of administrative convenience to the government. **I understand that I must show economic necessity and I will refer to the instructions concerning "Basic Criteria to Establish Economic Necessity."** **FEE REQUIRED.**

☐   (c) (16) - I entered the United States prior to January 1, 1972 and have been here since January 1, 1972. I have applied for registry as a lawful permanent resident alien and my application is pending. **FEE REQUIRED.**

☐   (c) (17) (i) - I am a (B-1) visitor for business. I am and have been (before coming to the United States) the domestic or personal servant for my employer who is temporarily in the United States. **FEE REQUIRED.**

☐   (c) (17) (ii) - I am a visitor for business (B-1) and am the employee of a foreign airline. I have B-1 nonimmigrant classification because I am unable to obtain visa classification as a treaty trader (E-1). **FEE REQUIRED.**

☐   (c) (18) - I am a deportable alien who has been placed under an order of supervision (OS). **I Understand that I must show economic necessity and I will refer to the instructions concerning "Basic Criteria to Establish Economic Necessity."** **FEE REQUIRED.**

☐   (c) (19) - I am an alien who is prima facie eligible for Temporary Protected Status (TPS) and (1) INS has not given me a reasonable chance to register during the first 30 days of the registration period [FEE REQUIRED], or (2) INS has not made a final decison as to my eligibility for TPS. **FEE REQUIRED.**

☆ U.S. GPO:1994-301-164/92697

INSTRUCTIONS

Please read carefully. An incomplete application may be returned to you, causing a delay in the processing of your application. If you need more space to complete an answer, add continuation sheets.

1. Can you file? You must be an eligible national of a foreign state (or parts thereof) that has been designated for Temporary Protected Status by the Attorney General pursuant to section 244A of the Immigration and Nationality Act. You should check with the nearest office of the Immigration and Naturalization Service for designations currently in force.

2. What documents do you need? *YOU DO NOT NEED TO PROVIDE ORIGINAL DOCUMENTS WITH THIS APPLICATION.* You must give INS copies of documents to prove you are a national of the country designated for Temporary Protected Status, your date of entry into the United States, and your residence in the United States.

    A.   INS may still require original documents from you in certain circumstances.

    B.   Copies of documents in a foreign language must be accompanied by a English translation. The translator must certify that the translation is accurate and that he or she is competent to translate.

    C.   Exception: If you are filing this application for annual registration/re-registration purposes (Part 1-2 on Form I-821) you do not have to submit any copies of documentation. You may, however, be asked for additional information and/or documentation in certain circumstances.

3. What documents do you need to prove identity and nationality? Any of the following:

    A.   Passport;

    B   Birth certificate accompanied by photo identification; or

    C.   Any national identity document from your country of origin bearing photo and/or fingerprint.

4. What documents do you need to prove date of entry into the United States? Any of the following:

    A.   Passport;

    B.   I-94 Arrival/Departure Record;

    C.   Copies of documents specified in item #5.

5. What documents do you need to prove residence in the United States? Any relevant documents such as:

    A.   Employment records (e.g. pay stubs, W-2 Forms, certification of the filing of Federal income tax returns, state verification of the filing of state income tax returns, letters from employer(s) or, if you are self employed, letters from banks and other firms with whom you have done business.

In all of the above, your name and the name of the employer or other interested organization must appear on the form or letter, as well as relevant dates. Letters from employers must be in affidavit form, and shall be signed and attested to by the employer under penalty of perjury. Such letters must include: (1) your address(es) at the time of employment; (2) Exact period(s) of employment; (3) Period(s) of layoff; (4) Duties with the company. If the records are unavailable, an affidavit form-letter stating that your employment records are unavailable and why such records are unavailable may be accepted. This affidavit form-letter shall be signed and attested to by the employer under penalty of perjury;

    B.   Rent receipts, utility bills (gas, electric, phone, etc.), receipts, or letters from companies showing the dates during which you received service;

    C.   School records (letters, report cards, etc.) from the schools that you or your children have attended in the United States showing name of school and periods of school attendance;

    D.   Hospital or medical records showing treatment or hospitalization of you or your children, showing the name of the medical facility or physician and the date(s) of the treatment or hospitalization;

    E.   Attestations by churches, unions, or other organizations to your residence by letter which: identify you by name; are signed by an official (whose title is shown); shows inclusive dates of membership; state the address where you resided during membership period; include the seal of the organization impressed on the letter or the letterhead of the organization, if the organization has letterhead stationery; establish how the author knows you; and establish the origin of the information being attested to;

    F.   Additional documents may include: money order receipts for money sent in or out of the country; passport entries; birth certificates of children born in the United States; bank books with dated transactions; correspondence between you and another person or organization; Social Security card; Selective Service card; automobile license receipts, title, vehicle registration, etc.; deeds, mortgages, contracts to which you have been a party; tax receipts; insurance policies, receipts, or letters; or

    G.   Any other relevant document.

6. What if documents are not available? If documents are not available, you can give INS an affidavit showing proof of unsuccessful efforts to obtain the documents, explaining why the consular process is unavailable (for identity documents), and affirming that you are a national of the designated state. Affidavits may also be used to help prove date of entry into the United States and residence in the United States. (INS may require a statement from the appropriate issuing authority certifying that the needed document is not available.) In addition to your own affidavit, written statements sworn to or affirmed by two persons who were living at the time and who have personal knowledge of the event you are trying to prove. The persons making the affidavits need not be citizens of the United States. Each affidavit should contain the following information regarding the person: his or her full name, address, date and place of birth, and his or her relationship to you, if any; full information concerning the event; and complete details concerning how the person acquired knowledge of the event.

7. What else is required to be submitted with this application?

    A.   Two completed and signed Fingerprint Cards, Form FD-258, if you are 14 years of age or older.

    B.   Two color photos of you taken within 30 days of the date of this application. The photo must have white backgrounds, must be glossy, unretouched, and not mounted. The dimension of the facial image should be about 1 inch from chin to top of hair in 3/4 frontal view, showing the right side of the face with the right ear visible. Using pencil or felt pen, lightly print name (and Alien Registration Number, if any) on the back of the photographs.

8. How should you prepare this form?

    A.   Type or print legibly in black or blue ink or ball point pen.

    B.   If you need extra space to complete any item, attach a continuation sheet, indicate the item number, and date and sign each sheet.

    C.   Answer all questions fully and accurately. If any item does not apply, please write "N/A"

9. Where should you file this form? The Service office having jurisdiction over your place of residence will accept this application either in person or through the mail or both. You should make inquiry of the Service office for filing instructions.

10. What is the fee? You must pay an application fee. The exact amount of the fee will be determined at the time the Attorney General designates nationals of a foreign state for Temporary Protected Status. All fees, except those presented when filing in person, must be in the form of a money order, cashier's check or certified bank check. NO PERSONAL CHECKS OF ANY TYPE WILL BE ACCEPTED. Cash is acceptable only when you present an application in person. DO NOT MAIL CASH. All money orders, cashier's checks or certified bank checks must be made payable in U.S. currency at a financial institution in the United States. Please assure that if a check or money order is drawn on the account of a person other than yourself, your name appears in the lower left corner on the face of the check or money order. If the check is not honored, INS will charge you $5.00.

Make the check or money order payable to "Immigration and Naturalization Service". However,

    A.   if you live in Guam: Make the check or money order payable to "Treasurer, Guam", or

    B.   if you live in the U.S. Virgin Islands: Make the check or money order payable to "Commissioner of Finance of the Virgin Islands".

11. Employment Authorization and Travel.

    A.   Form I-765 is required for all TPS applicants, regardless of age, and regardless of whether employment authorization is desired, since the I-765 is the data entry document for the Temporary Protected Status Program. You may be charged a fee for the filing of the I-765 depending on the differing statutory and regulatory requirements that apply to you.

    B.   If your application for Temporary Protected Status is granted and you desire to travel outside the United States and return you must request advance parole from the district director having jurisdiction over your residence and pay the prescribed fee. Form I-512 will be issued to you if your request for advance parole is granted.

12. May the filing fees for Form I-821 and I-765 be waived? Yes. If you are poor and unable to pay the filing fees, 8 C.F.R. 103.7(c) provides that you may apply for a waiver of the filing fees. In order to obtain a fee waiver, you must submit with these forms a written statement, made under oath, affirmation or, pursuant to 28 U.S.C. 1746, under penalty of perjury. In the written statement you must indicate that you believe you are eligible for Temporary Protected Status and that you want to have the filing fees waived. You must also indicate why you are unable to pay the required fees.

13. What is our authority for collecting this information? We request the information on the form to carry out the immigration laws contained in Title 8, United States Code, Section 1154(a). We need this information to determine whether you are eligible for immigration benefits. The information you provide may also be disclosed to other federal, state, local, and foreign law enforcement and regulatory agencies. You do not have to give this information. However, if you do not give some or all of it, your application may be denied.

14. Reporting Burden. Public reporting burden for this information collection is estimated to average 1 hour and 30 minutes computed as follows: 1) learning about the form, and understanding the instructions, 30 minutes; 2) collecting the necessary supporting documents 15 minutes; 3) completing the form, 15 minutes; and 4) traveling to and waiting at a preparer's office (e.g. attorney or voluntary agency), 30 minutes. If you have comments regarding the accuracy of this estimate, or suggestions for making this form simpler, you can write to both the Immigration and Naturalization Service, 425 I Street, N.W.; Room 5304, Washington, D.C. 20536; and the Office of Management and Budget, Paperwork Reduction Project, OMB No. 1115-0170, Washington, D.C. 20503.

START HERE - Please Type or Print

FOR INS USE ONLY

Part 1. Type of Application *(check one)*	Remarks

1. _________ This is my first application to register for Temporary Protected Status.
2. _________ This is my application for annual registration/re-registration. I have previously been granted Temporary Protected Status. I have maintained and continue to maintain the conditions of eligibility for Temporary Protected Status.

Part 2. Information about You

Family Name | First | Middle Initial

U.S. Mailing Address - Care of

Street Number and Name | Apt. #

Town/City | County

State | ZIP Code

Place of Birth (Town or City) | (State/Country)

Country of Residence | Country of Citizenship

Date of Birth *(month/day/year)* | Sex ☐ Male ☐ Female

Marital Status ☐Single ☐Divorced ☐Married ☐Widowed | Other Names Used *(including maiden name)*

Date of entry into the U.S. | Place of entry into the U.S.

Manner of Arrival *(Visitor, student, stowaway, without inspection, etc.)*

Arrival/Departure Record (I-94) Number | Date authorized stay expired/or will expire, as shown on form I-94 or I-95

Your current immigration Status

In Status *(state nonimmigrant classification e.g. F-1, etc.)*

Out of Status *(state nonimmigrant violation e.g. overstay student etc.; EWI)*

Alien Registration Number *(If any)* | Social Security Number

Are you now or have you ever been under immigration proceedings?
☐ Yes ☐ No Where_________________ When_________________
☐ Exclusion ☐ Deportation ☐ Rescission ☐ Judicial Proceedings

Action Stamp

Fee Stamp

Case ID#:

A#:

Part 3. Information about Your spouse and children *(if any)*

Name of Spouse Last | First | Middle Initial

Address (number and street) | Apt #

Town/City | State

Country | Zip/Postal Code

To Be Completed by
***Attorney or Representative*, if any**
☐ Fill in box if G-28 is attached to represent the applicant

VOLAG#

ATTY State License #

Form I-821 (Rev. 5/22/91)N   ***Continued on back.***

Date of Birth (*month/day/ year*)	Date and Place of Present Marriage
Name of prior husbands/wives	Date(s) Marriage(s) Ended

List the names, ages, and current residence of any children

Name - (Last)	(First)	(Middle Initial)	Date of Birth	Residence

Part 4.   **Eligibility Standards**

1.   Fill in the necessary information:

I am a national of the foreign state of _________________ , and I entered the United States on _______________________________ , and I have resided in the United States since that time.

2.   To be eligible for Temporary Protected Status, you must be admissible as an immigrant to the United States, with certain exceptions. Do any of the following apply to you?

a.   have you been convicted of any felony or 2 or more misdemeanors committed in the United States;

b.   (i) have you ordered, incited, assisted, or otherwise participated in the persecution of any person on account of race, religion, nationality, membership in a particular social group or political opinion;

(ii) have you been convicted by a final judgment of a particularly serious crime, constituting a danger to the community of the United States (an alien convicted of an aggravated felony is considered to have committed a particularly serious crime);

(iii) have you committed a serious nonpolitical crime outside of the United States prior to your arrival in the United States; or

(iv) have you engaged in or are you still engaged in activities that could be reasonable grounds for concluding that you are a danger to the security of the United States;

c.   (i) have you been convicted of, or have you committed acts which constitute the essential elements of a crime (other than a purely political offense) or a violation of or a conspiracy to violate any law relating to a controlled substance as defined in Section 102 of the Controlled Substance Act;

(ii) have you been convicted of 2 or more offenses (other than purely political offenses) for which the aggregate sentences to confinement actually imposed were 5 years or more;

(iii) have you trafficked in or do you continue to traffic in any controlled substance or are or have been a knowing assister, abettor, conspirator, or colluder with others in the illicit trafficking of any controlled substance;

(iv) have you engaged or do you continue to engage solely, principally, or incidentally in any activity related to espionage or sabotage or violate any law involving the export of goods, technology, or sensitive information, any other unlawful activity, or any activity the purpose of which is in opposition, or the control, or overthrow of the government of the United States;

Form I-821 (Rev. 05/22/91)   *Continued on next page*

(v) have you engaged in or do you continue to engage in terrorist activities;

(vi) have you engaged in or do you continue to engage or plan to engage in activities in the United States that would have potentially serious adverse foreign policy consequences for the United States;

(vii) have you been or do you continue to be a member of the Communist or other totalitarian party, except when membership was involuntary; and

(viii) have you participated in Nazi persecution or genocide.

d.   have you been arrested, cited, charged, indicted, fined, or imprisoned for breaking or violating any law or ordinance, excluding traffic violations, or been the beneficiary of a pardon, amnesty, rehabilitation decree, other act of clemency or similar action;

e.   have you committed a serious criminal offense in the United States and asserted immunity from prosecution;

f.   have you within the past 10 years engaged in prostitution or procurement of prostitution or do you continue to engage in prostitution or procurement of prostitution;

g.   have you been or do you intend to be involved in any other commercial vice;

h.   have you been excluded and deported from the United States within the past year, or have you been deported or removed from the United States at government expense within the last 5 years (20 years if you have been convicted of an aggravated felony);

i   have you ever assisted any other person to enter the United States in violation of the law;

j   (i) do you have a communicable disease of public health significance,

(ii) do you have or have you had a physical or mental disorder and behavior (or a history of behavior that is likely to recur) associated with the disorder which has posed or may pose a threat to the property, safety or welfare of yourself or others;

(iii) are you now or have you been a drug abuser or drug addict;

k.   have you entered the United States as a stowaway;

l.   are you subject to a final order for violation of section 274C (producing and/or using false documentation to unlawfully satisfy a requirement of the Immigration and Nationality Act);

m.   do you practice polygamy;

n.   were you the guardian of, and did you accompany another alien who was ordered excluded and deported from the United States;

o.   have you detained, retained, or withheld the custody of a child, having a lawful claim to United States citizenship, outside the United States from a United States citizen granted custody.

If any of the above statements apply to you, indicate which one(s) by number reference on the line below (for example "2 k") and include a full explanation on a separate piece of paper. If you were ever arrested you should provide the disposition (outcome) of the arrest (for example, "case dismissed") from the appropriate authority.

PLEASE NOTE: If you placed any of the following numbered references on the line above you may be eligible for a waiver of the grounds described in the statements: 2e; 2f; 2g; 2h; 2i; 2j; 2k; 2l; 2m; 2n; 2o. Form I-601 or I-724 are the Service forms used to request a waiver. These forms are available at INS offices.

134

Part 5.   Your Certification

Your Certification: I certify, under penalty of perjury under the laws of the United States of America, that the foregoing is true and correct. Copies of documents submitted are exact photocopies of unaltered original documents and I understand that I may be required to submit original documents to the INS at a later date. Furthermore, I authorize the release of any information from my records which the Immigration and Naturalization Service needs to determine eligibility for the benefit that I am seeking.

Signature:_________________________________Date:_________________Telephone No.: _______________________________

Signature of Person Preparing Form if other than above:

I declare that I prepared this document at the request of the person above and that it is based on all information of which I have any knowledge.

Print Name: _____________________________________Signature:____Date:_______________

Address:____

Part 6.   Checklist

_____ Have you answered each question?
_____ Have you signed the application?

Have you enclosed:

_____The filing fee for this application or a written request for a waiver of the filing fee (see instructions, item 12)?

_____Supporting evidence to prove identity, nationality, date of entry and residence?

_____Other required supporting documents (fingerprint charts, pictures etc.) for each application?

IT IS NOT POSSIBLE TO COVER ALL THE CONDITIONS FOR ELIGIBILITY OR TO GIVE INSTRUCTIONS FOR EVERY SITUATION. IF YOU HAVE CAREFULLY READ ALL THE INSTRUCTIONS AND STILL HAVE QUESTIONS, PLEASE CONTACT YOUR NEAREST INS OFFICE. IT IS RECOMMENDED THAT YOU KEEP A COMPLETE COPY OF THIS APPLICATION FOR YOUR RECORDS.

Form I-821 (Rev. 05/22/91)

U.S. IMMIGRATION & NATURALIZATION SERVICE

COLOR PHOTOGRAPH SPECIFICATIONS

◀ SAMPLE PHOTOGRAPH

HEAD SIZE (INCLUDING HAIR) ▶
MUST FIT INSIDE OVAL

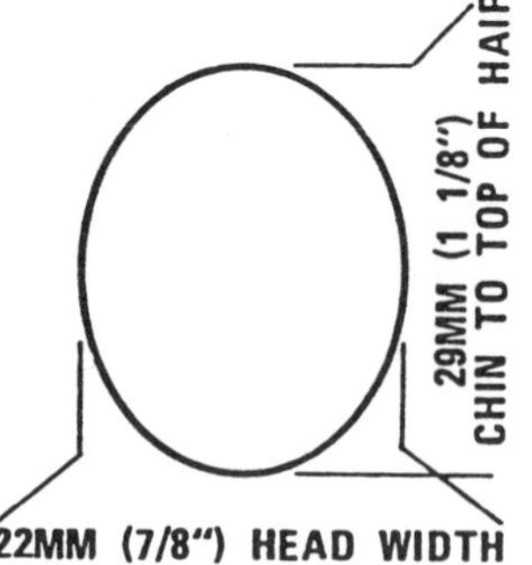

COLOR FILMS OF THE INTEGRAL TYPE, NON-PEEL-APART, ARE UNACCEPTABLE. THESE ARE EASILY RECOGNIZED AS THE BACK OF THE FILMS ARE BLACK. THE ACCEPTABLE INSTANT COLOR FILM HAS A WHITE BACKING.

- PHOTOGRAPH MUST SHOW THE SUBJECT IN A ¾ FRONTAL PORTRAIT AS SHOWN ABOVE

- RIGHT EAR MUST BE EXPOSED IN PHOTOGRAPH FOR ALL APPLICANTS, HATS MUST NOT BE WORN.

- PHOTOGRAPH OUTER DIMENSION **MUST** BE LARGER THAN 1¹/₄ W x 1³/₈ H, BUT HEAD SIZE, (INCLUDING HAIR) **MUST** FIT WITHIN THE ILLUSTRATED OVAL (OUTER DIMENSION DOES NOT INCLUDE BORDER IF ONE IS USED)

- PHOTOGRAPH MUST BE COLOR WITH A WHITE BACKGROUND EQUAL IN REFLECTANCE TO BOND TYPING PAPER

- SURFACE OF THE PHOTOGRAPH **MUST BE GLOSSY**

- PHOTOGRAPH MUST NOT BE STAINED, CRACKED, OR MUTILATED, AND MUST LIE FLAT

- PHOTOGRAPHIC IMAGE MUST BE SHARP AND CORRECTLY EXPOSED, PHOTOGRAPH MUST BE UN-RETOUCHED

- PHOTOGRAPHS MUST NOT BE PASTED ON CARDS OR MOUNTED IN ANY WAY

- **2 (TWO)** PHOTOGRAPHS OF EVERY APPLICANT, REGARDLESS OF AGE, MUST BE SUBMITTED

- PHOTOGRAPHS MUST BE TAKEN WITHIN THIRTY (30) DAYS OF APPLICATION DATE

- SNAPSHOTS, GROUP PICTURES, OR FULL LENGTH PORTRAITS **WILL NOT** BE ACCEPTED

- USING CRAYON OR FELT PEN, TO AVOID MUTILATION OF THE PHOTOGRAPHS, **LIGHTLY** PRINT YOUR NAME (AND ALIEN REGISTRATION RECEIPT NUMBER IF KNOWN) ON THE BACK OF ALL PHOTOGRAPHS

- **IMPORTANT NOTE** - FAILURE TO SUBMIT PHOTOGRAPHS IN COMPLIANCE WITH THESE SPECIFICATIONS WILL DELAY THE PROCESSING OF YOUR APPLICATION

SAMPLES OF UNACCEPTABLE PHOTOGRAPHS

FACING WRONG WAY

HEAD SIZE TOO LARGE

HEAD SIZE TOO SMALL

DARK BACKGROUND

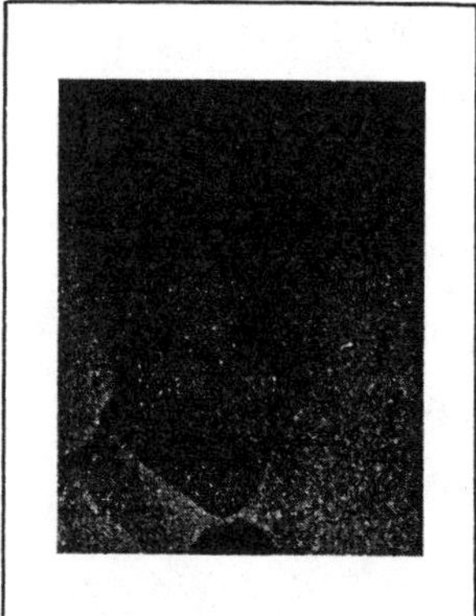

TOO DARK

TOO LIGHT

LIST OF 100 STANDARDIZED QUESTIONS
U.S. GOVERNMENT AND HISTORY

1. What are the colors of our flag?

2. How many stars are there in our flag?

3. What color are the stars of our flag?

4. What do the stars on the flag mean?

5. How may stripes are there in the flag?

6. What color are the stripes?

7. What do the stripes on the flag mean?

8. How many states are there in the Union?

9. What is the 4th of July?

10. What is the date of Independence Day?

11. Independence from whom?

12. What country did we fight during the Revolutionary War?

13. Who was the first president of the United States?

14. Who is the president of the United States today?

15. Who is the vice-president of the United States today?

16. Who elects the president of the United States?

17. Who becomes the president of the United States if the president should die?

18. For how long do we elect the president?

19. What is the Constitution?

20. Can the Constitution be changed?

21. What do we call a change to the Constitution?

22. How may changes or amendments are there to the Constitution?

23. How may branches are there in our government?

24. What are the three branches of our government?

25. What is the legislative branch of our government?

26. Who makes the laws in the United States?

27. What is Congress?

28. What are the duties of Congress?

29. Who elects Congress?

30. How many senators are there in Congress?

31. Can you name the two senators from your state?

32. For how long do we elect each senator?

33. How many representatives are there in Congress?

34. For how long do we elect the representatives?

35. What is the executive branch of our government?

36. What is the judiciary branch of our government?

37. What are the duties of the Supreme Court?

38. What is the supreme law of the United States?

39. What is the Bill of Rights?

40. What is the capital of your state?

41. Who is the current governor of your state?

42. Who becomes president of the United States if the president and the vice-president should die?

43. Who is the Chief Justice of the Supreme Court?

44. Can you name the 13 original states?

45. Who said, "Give me liberty or give me death"?

46. Which countries were our enemies during World War II?

47. What are the 49th and 50th states of the Union?

48. How many terms can a president serve?

49. Who was Martin Luther King, Jr.?

50. Who is the head of your local government?

51. According to the Constitution, a person must meet certain requirements in order to be eligible to become President. Name one of these requirements.

52. Why are there 100 senators in the Senate?

53. Who selects the Supreme Court Justices?

54. How may Supreme Court justices are there?

55. Why did the Pilgrims come to America?

56. What is the head executive of a state government called?

57. What is the head executive of a city government called?

58. What holiday was celebrated for the first time by the American colonists?

59. Who was the main writer of the Declaration of Independence?

60. When was the Declaration of Independence adopted?

61. What was the basic belief of the Declaration of Independence?

62. What is the national anthem of the United States?

63. Who wrote the Star-Spangled Banner?

64. Where does freedom of speech come from?

65. What is the minimum voting age in the United States?

66. Who signs bills into law?

67. What is the highest court in the United States?

68. Who was the president during the Civil War?

69. What did the Emancipation Proclamation do?

70. What special group advises the president?

71. Which president is called the "Father of our Country"?

72. What Immigration and Naturalization Service form is used to apply to become a naturalized citizen?

73. Who helped the Pilgrims in America?

74. What is the name of the ship that brought the Pilgrims to America?

75. What were the 13 original states of the United States called?

 76. Name three rights or freedoms guaranteed by the Bill of Rights?

77. Who has the power to declare war?

78. What kind of government does the United States have?

79. Which president freed the slaves?

80. In what year was the Constitution written?

81. What are the first ten amendments to the Constitution called?

82. Name one purpose of the United Nations.

83. Where does Congress meet?

84. Whose rights are guaranteed by the Constitution and the Bill of Rights?

85. What is the introduction to the Constitution called?

86. Name one benefit of being a citizen of the United States.

87. What is the most important right granted to United States citizens?

88. What is the Unites States Capitol?

89. What is the White House?

90. Where is the White House located?

91. What is the name of the president's official home?

92. Name one right guaranteed by the first amendment.

93. Who is the Commander in Chief of the United States military?

94. Which president was the first Commander in Chief of the United States military?

95. In what month do we vote for the president?

96. In what month is the new president inaugurated?

97. How many times may a senator be re-elected?

98. How may times may a congressman be re-elected?

99. What are the two major political parties in the United States?

100. How may states are there in the United States?

ANSWERS TO THE 100 STANDARDIZED QUESTIONS
U.S. GOVERNMENT AND HISTORY

1. Red, white and blue.
2. 50.
3. White.
4. One for each state in the Union.
5. 13.
6. Red and white.
7. They represent the 13 original states.
8. 50.
9. Independence Day.
10. July 4th.
11. England.
12. England.
13. George Washington.
14. Bill Clinton (current).
15. Al Gore (current).
16. The electoral college.
17. Vice-President.
18. Four years.
19. The supreme law of the land.
20. Yes.
21. Amendments.
22. 26.
23. Three.
24. Legislative, Executive and Judicial.
25. Congress.
26. Congress.
27. The Senate and the House of Representatives.
28. To make laws.
29. The people.
30. 100.
31. (insert local information).
32. Six years.
33. 435.
34. Two years.
35. The President, Cabinet, and Departments under the Cabinet members.
36. The Supreme Court.
37. To interpret laws.
38. The constitution.

39. The first ten amendments of the Constitution.

40. (insert local information).

41. (insert local information).

42. Speaker of the House of Representatives.

43. William Rehnquist.

44. Connecticut, New Hampshire, New York, New Jersey, Massachusetts, Pennsylvania, Delaware, Virginia, North Carolina, Sout Carolina, Georgia, Rhode Island, and Maryland.

45. Patrick Henry.

46. Germany, Italy, and Japan.

47. Hawaii and Alaska.

48. Two.

49. A civil rights leader.

50. (insert local information).

51. Must be a natural born citizen of the United States; Must be at least 35 years old by the time he/she will serve; Must have lived in the United States for at least 14 years.

52. Two from each state.

53. Appointed by the president.

54. Nine.

55. For religious freedom.

56. Governor.

57. Mayor.

58. Thanksgiving.

59. Thomas Jefferson.

60. July 4, 1776.

61. That all men are created equal.

62. The Star-Spangled Banner.

63. Francis Scott Key.

64. The Bill of Rights.

65. Eighteen.

66. The President.

67. The Supreme Court.

68. Abraham Lincoln.

69. Freed many slaves.

70. The Cabinet.

71. George Washington.

72. Form N-400, "Application to File Petition for Naturalization".

73. The American Indians (Native Americans)

74. The Mayflower.

75. Colonies.

76. 1) The right or freedom of speech, press, religion, peaceable assembly and requesting change of government.

2) The right to bear arms (the right to have weapons or own a gun, though subject to certain regulations).

3) The government may not quarter, or house, soldiers in the people's homes during peacetime without the people's consent.

4) The government may not search or take a person's property without a warrant.

5) A person may not be tried twice for the same crime and does not have to testify against him/herself.

6) A person charged with a crime still has some rights, such as the right to a trial and to have a lawyer.

7) The right to trial by jury in most cases.

8) Protection against excessive or unreasonable fines or cruel and unusual punishment.

9) The people have rights other than those mentioned in the Constitution.

10) Any power not given to the federal government by the Constitution is a power of either the state or the people.

77. Congress.

78. Democracy.

79. Abraham Lincoln.

80. 1787.

81. The Bill of Rights.

82. For countries to discuss and try to resolve world problems; to provide economic aid to many countries.

83. In the Capitol in Washington, D.C.

84. Everyone (citizens and non-citizens living in the United States).

85. The Preamble.

86. Obtain federal government jobs; travel with a United States passport; petition for close relatives to come to the United States to live.

87. The right to vote.

88. The place where Congress meets.

89. The President's official home.

90. Washington, D.C. (1600 Pennsylvania Avenue, N.W.)

91. The White House.

92. Freedom of: speech, press, religion, peaceable assembly, and requesting change of the government.

93. The president.

94. George Washington.

95. November.

96. January.

97. There is no limit.

98. There is no limit.

99. Democrat and Republican.

100. Fifty.

Oath of Allegiance

"I hereby declare, on oath, that I absolutely and entirely renounce and abjure all allegiance and fidelity to any foreign prince, potentate, state or sovereignty, of whom or which I have heretofore been a subject or citizen; that I will support and defend the Constitution and laws of the United States of America against all enemies, foreign and domestic; that I will bear true faith and allegiance to the same; that I will bear arms on behalf of the United States when required by the law; that I will perform noncombatant service in the armed forces of the United States when required by the law; that I will perform work of national importance under civilian direction when required by the law; and that I take this obligation freely without any mental reservation or purpose of evasion; so help me God."

How To Save On Attorney Fees

M illions of Americans know they need legal protection, whether it's to get agreements in writing, protect themselves from lawsuits, or document business transactions. But too often these basic but important legal matters are neglected because of something else millions of Americans know: legal services are expensive.

They don't have to be. In response to the demand for affordable legal protection and services, there are now specialized clinics that process simple documents. Paralegals help people prepare legal claims on a freelance basis. People find they can handle their own legal affairs with do-it-yourself legal guides and kits. Indeed, this book is a part of this growing trend.

When are these alternatives to a lawyer appropriate? If you hire an attorney, how can you make sure you're getting good advice for a reasonable fee? Most importantly, do you know how to lower your legal expenses?

When there is no alternative

Make no mistake: serious legal matters require a lawyer. The tips in this book can help you reduce your legal fees, but there is no alternative to good professional legal services in certain circumstances:

- When you are charged with a felony, you are a repeat offender, or jail is possible.
- When a substantial amount of money or property is at stake in a lawsuit.
- When you are a party in an adversarial divorce or custody case.
- When you are an alien facing deportation.

- When you are the plaintiff in a personal injury suit that involves large sums of money.
- When you're involved in very important transactions.

Are you sure you want to take it to court?

Consider the following questions before you pursue legal action:

 *What are your financial resources?*

Money buys experienced attorneys, and experience wins over first-year lawyers and public defenders. Even with a strong case, you may save money by not going to court. Yes, people win millions in court. But for every big winner there are ten plaintiffs who either lose or win so little that litigation wasn't worth their effort.

 *Do you have the time and energy for a trial?*

Courts are overbooked, and by the time your case is heard your initial zeal may have grown cold. If you can, make a reasonable settlement out of court. On personal matters, like a divorce or custody case, consider the emotional toll on all parties. Any legal case will affect you in some way. You will need time away from work. A newsworthy case may bring press coverage. Your loved ones, too, may face publicity. There is usually good reason to settle most cases quickly, quietly, and economically.

 *How can you settle your disputes without litigation?*

Consider *mediation.* In mediation, each party pays half the mediator's fee and, together, they attempt to work out a compromise informally. *Binding arbitration* is another alternative. For a small fee, a trained specialist serves as judge, hears both sides, and hands down a ruling that both parties have agreed to accept.

So you need an attorney

Having done your best to avoid litigation, if you still find yourself headed for court, you will need an attorney. To get the right attorney at a reasonable cost, be guided by these four questions:

What type of case is it?

You don't seek a foot doctor for a toothache. Find an attorney experienced in your type of legal problem. If you can get recommendations from clients who have recently won similar cases, do so.

Highlight

Even with a strong case, you may save money by not going to court.

 *Where will the trial be held?*

You want a lawyer familiar with that court system and one who knows the court personnel and the local protocol – which can vary from one locality to another.

 *Should you hire a large or small firm?*

Hiring a senior partner at a large and prestigious law firm sounds reassuring, but chances are the actual work will be handled by associates – at high rates. Small firms may give your case more attention but, with fewer resources, take longer to get the work done.

 *What can you afford?*

Hire an attorney you can afford, of course, but know what a fee quote includes. High fees may reflect a firm's luxurious offices, high-paid staff and unmonitored expenses, while low estimates may mean "unexpected" costs later. Ask for a written estimate of all costs and anticipated expenses.

How to find a good lawyer

Whether you need an attorney quickly or you're simply open to future possibilities, here are seven nontraditional methods for finding your lawyer:

1. *Word of mouth:* Successful lawyers develop reputations. Your friends, business associates and other professionals are potential referral sources. But beware of hiring a friend. Keep the client-attorney relationship strictly business.

2. *Directories:* The Yellow Pages and the Martin-Hubbell Lawyer Directory (in your local library) can help you locate a lawyer with the right education, background and expertise for your case.

3. *Databases:* A paralegal should be able to run a quick computer search of local attorneys for you using the Westlaw or Lexis database.

4. *State bar association:* Bar associations are listed in phone books. Along with lawyer referrals, your bar association can direct you to low-cost legal clinics or specialists in your area.

5. *Law schools:* Did you know that a legal clinic run by a law school gives law students hands-on experience? This may fit your legal needs. A third-year law student loaded with enthusiasm and a little experience might fill the bill quite inexpensively – or even for free.

6. *Advertisements:* Ads are a lawyer's business card. If a "TV attorney" seems to have a good track record with your kind of case, why not call? Just don't be swayed by the glamour of a high-

profile attorney.

7. *Your own ad:* A small ad describing the qualifications and legal expertise you're seeking, placed in a local bar association journal, may get you just the lead you need.

How to hire and work with your attorney

No matter how you hear about an attorney, you must interview him or her in person. Call the office during business hours and ask to speak to the attorney directly. Then explain your case briefly and mention how you obtained the attorney's name. If the attorney sounds interested and knowledgeable, arrange for a visit.

The ten-point visit:

1. Note the address. This is a good indication of the rates to expect.

2. Note the condition of the offices. File-laden desks and poorly maintained work space may indicate a poorly run firm.

3. Look for up-to-date computer equipment and an adequate complement of support personnel.

4. Note the appearance of the attorney. How will he or she impress a judge or jury?

5. Is the attorney attentive? Does the attorney take notes, ask questions, follow up on points you've mentioned?

6. Ask what schools he or she has graduated from, and feel free to check credentials with the state bar association.

7. Does the attorney have a good track record with your type of case?

8. Does he or she explain legal terms to you in plain English?

9. Are the firm's costs reasonable?

10. Will the attorney provide references?

Hiring the attorney

Having chosen your attorney, make sure all the terms are agreeable. Send letters to any other attorneys you have interviewed, thanking them for their time and interest in your case and explaining that you have retained another attorney's services.

Highlight

Explain your case briefly and mention how you obtained the attorney's name. If the attorney sounds interested and knowledgeable, arrange for a visit.

Request a letter from your new attorney outlining your retainer agreement. The letter should list all fees you will be responsible for as well as the billing arrangement. Did you arrange to pay in installments? This should be noted in your retainer agreement.

Controlling legal costs

Legal fees and expenses can get out of control easily, but the client who is willing to put in the effort can keep legal costs manageable. Work out a budget with your attorney. Create a timeline for your case. Estimate the costs involved in each step.

Legal fees can be straightforward. Some lawyers charge a fixed rate for a specific project. Others charge contingency fees (they collect a percentage of your recovery, usually 35-50 percent, if you win and nothing if you lose). But most attorneys prefer to bill by the hour. Expenses can run the gamut, with one hourly charge for taking depositions and another for making copies.

Have your attorney give you a list of charges for services rendered and an itemized monthly bill. The bill should explain the service performed, who performed the work, when the service was provided, how long it took, and how the service benefits your case.

Ample opportunity abounds in legal billing for dishonesty and greed. There is also plenty of opportunity for knowledgeable clients to cut their bills significantly if they know what to look for. Asking the right questions and setting limits on fees is smart and can save you a bundle. Don't be afraid to question legal bills. It's your case and your money!

When the bill arrives

- *Retainer fees:* You should already have a written retainer agreement. Ideally, the retainer fee applies toward case costs, and your agreement puts that in writing. Protect yourself by escrowing the retainer fee until the case has been handled to your satisfaction.

- *Office visit charges:* Track your case and all documents, correspondence, and bills. Diary all dates, deadlines and questions you want to ask your attorney during your next office visit. This keeps expensive office visits focused and productive, with more accomplished in less time. If your attorney charges less for phone consultations than office visits, reserve visits for those tasks that must be done in person.

- *Phone bills:* This is where itemized bills are essential. Who made the call, who was spoken to, what was discussed, when was the call made, and how long did it last? Question any charges that seem unnecessary or excessive (over 60 minutes).

- *Administrative costs:* Your case may involve hundreds, if not thousands, of documents: motions, affidavits, depositions, interrogatories, bills, memoranda, and letters. Are they all necessary? Understand your attorney's case strategy before paying for an endless stream of costly documents.

- *Associate and paralegal fees:* Note in your retainer agreement which staff people will have access to your file. Then you'll have an informed and efficient staff working on your case, and you'll recognize their names on your bill. Of course, your attorney should handle the important part of your case, but less costly paralegals or associates may handle routine matters more economically. Note: Some firms expect their associates to meet a quota of billable hours, although the time spent is not always warranted. Review your bill. Does the time spent make sense for the document in question? Are several staff involved in matters that should be handled by one person? Don't be afraid to ask questions. And withhold payment until you have satisfactory answers.

- *Court stenographer fees:* Depositions and court hearings require costly transcripts and stenographers. This means added expenses. Keep an eye on these costs.

- *Copying charges:* Your retainer fee should limit the number of copies made of your complete file. This is in your legal interest, because multiple files mean multiple chances others may access your confidential information. It is also in your financial interest, because copying costs can be astronomical.

- *Fax costs:* As with the phone and copier, the fax can easily run up costs. Set a limit.

- *Postage charges:* Be aware of how much it costs to send a legal document overnight, or a registered letter. Offer to pick up or deliver expensive items when it makes sense.

- *Filing fees:* Make it clear to your attorney that you want to minimize the number of court filings in your case. Watch your bill and question any filing that seems unnecessary.

- *Document production fee:* Turning over documents to your

Highlight

Note in your retainer agreement which staff people will have access to your file. Then you'll have an informed and efficient staff working on your case, and you'll recognize their names on your bill.

opponent is mandatory and expensive. If you're faced with reproducing boxes of documents, consider having the job done by a commercial firm rather than your attorney's office.

- *Research and investigations:* Pay only for photographs that can be used in court. Can you hire a photographer at a lower rate than what your attorney charges? Reserve that right in your retainer agreement. Database research can also be extensive and expensive; if your attorney uses Westlaw or Nexis, set limits on the research you will pay for.

- *Expert witnesses:* Question your attorney if you are expected to pay for more than a reasonable number of expert witnesses. Limit the number to what is essential to your case.

- *Technology costs:* Avoid videos, tape recordings, and graphics if you can use old-fashioned diagrams to illustrate your case.

- *Travel expenses:* Travel expenses for those connected to your case can be quite costly unless you set a maximum budget. Check all travel-related items on your bill, and make sure they are appropriate. Always question why the travel is necessary before you agree to pay for it.

- *Appeals costs:* Losing a case often means an appeal, but weigh the costs involved before you make that decision. If money is at stake, do a cost-benefit analysis to see if an appeal is financially justified.

- *Monetary damages:* Your attorney should be able to help you estimate the total damages you will have to pay if you lose a civil case. Always consider settling out of court rather than proceeding to trial when the trial costs will be high.

- *Surprise costs:* Surprise costs are so routine they're predictable. The judge may impose unexpected court orders on one or both sides, or the opposition will file an unexpected motion that increases your legal costs. Budget a few thousand dollars over what you estimate your case will cost. It usually is needed.

- *Padded expenses:* Assume your costs and expenses are legitimate. But some firms do inflate expenses – office supplies, database searches, copying, postage, phone bills – to bolster their bottom line. Request copies of bills your law firm receives from support services. If you are not the only client represented on a bill, determine those charges related to your case.

Keeping it legal without a lawyer

The best way to save legal costs is to avoid legal problems. There are hundreds of ways to decrease your chances of lawsuits and other nasty legal encounters. Most simply involve a little common sense. You can also use your own initiative to find and use the variety of self-help legal aid available to consumers.

11 situations in which you may not need a lawyer

1. *No-fault divorce:* Married couples with no children, minimal property, and no demands for alimony can take advantage of divorce mediation services. A lawyer should review your divorce agreement before you sign it, but you will have saved a fortune in attorney fees. A marital or family counselor may save a seemingly doomed marriage, or help both parties move beyond anger to a calm settlement. Either way, counseling can save you money.

2. *Wills:* Do-it-yourself wills and living trusts are ideal for people with estates of less than $600,000. Even if an attorney reviews your final documents, a will kit allows you to read the documents, ponder your bequests, fill out sample forms, and discuss your wishes with your family at your leisure, without a lawyer's meter running.

3. *Incorporating:* Incorporating a small business can be done by any business owner. Your state government office provides the forms and instructions necessary. A visit to your state offices will probably be necessary to perform a business name check. A fee of $100-$200 is usually charged for processing your Articles of Incorporation. The rest is paperwork: filling out forms correctly; holding regular, official meetings; and maintaining accurate records.

4. *Routine business transactions:* Copyrights, for example, can be applied for by asking the US Copyright Office for the appropriate forms and brochures. The same is true of the US Patent and Trademark Office. If your business does a great deal of document preparation and research, hire a certified paralegal rather than paying an attorney's rates. Consider mediation or binding arbitration rather than going to court for a business dispute. Hire

Highlight

The best way to save legal costs is to avoid legal problems.

a human resources/benefits administrator to head off disputes concerning discrimination or other employee charges.

5. *Repairing bad credit:* When money matters get out of hand, attorneys and bankruptcy should not be your first solution. Contact a credit counseling organization that will help you work out manageable payment plans so that everyone wins. It can also help you learn to manage your money better. A good company to start with is the Consumer Credit Counseling Service, 1-800-388-2227.

6. *Small Claims Court:* For legal grievances amounting to a few thousand dollars in damages, represent yourself in Small Claims Court. There is a small filing fee, forms to fill out, and several court visits necessary. If you can collect evidence, state your case in a clear and logical presentation, and come across as neat, respectful and sincere, you can succeed in Small Claims Court.

7. *Traffic Court:* Like Small Claims Court, Traffic Court may show more compassion to a defendant appearing without an attorney. If you are ticketed for a minor offense and want to take it to court, you will be asked to plead guilty or not guilty. If you plead guilty, you can ask for leniency in sentencing by presenting mitigating circumstances. Bring any witnesses who can support your story, and remember that presentation (some would call it acting ability) is as important as fact.

8. *Residential zoning petition:* If a homeowner wants to open a home business, build an addition, or make other changes that may affect his or her neighborhood, town approval is required. But you don't need a lawyer to fill out a zoning variance application, turn it in, and present your story at a public hearing. Getting local support before the hearing is the best way to assure a positive vote; contact as many neighbors as possible to reassure them that your plans won't adversely affect them or the neighborhood.

9. *Government benefit applications:* Applying for veterans' or unemployment benefits may be daunting, but the process doesn't require legal help. Apply for either immediately upon becoming eligible. Note: If your former employer contests your application for unemployment benefits and you have to defend yourself at a hearing, you may want to consider hiring an attorney.

10. ***Receiving government files:*** The Freedom of Information Act gives every American the right to receive copies of government information about him or her. Write a letter to the appropriate state or federal agency, noting the precise information you want. List each document in a separate paragraph. Mention the Freedom of Information Act, and state that you will pay any expenses. Close with your signature and the address the documents should be sent to. An approved request may take six months to arrive. If it is refused on the grounds that the information is classified or violates another's privacy, send a letter of appeal explaining why the released information would not endanger anyone. Enlist the support of your local state or federal representative, if possible, to smooth the approval process.

11. ***Citizenship:*** Arriving in the United States to work and become a citizen is a process tangled in bureaucratic red tape, but it requires more perseverance than legal assistance. Immigrants can learn how to obtain a "Green Card," under what circumstances they can work, and what the requirements of citizenship are by contacting the Immigration Services or reading a good self-help book.

Highlight

Arriving in the United States to work and become a citizen is a process tangled in bureaucratic red tape, but it requires more perseverance than legal assistance.

Save more; it's E-Z

When it comes to saving attorneys' fees, E-Z Legal Forms is the consumer's best friend. America's largest publisher of self-help legal products offers legally valid forms for virtually every situation. E-Z Legal Kits and E-Z Legal Guides include all necessary forms with a simple-to-follow manual of instructions or a layman's book. E-Z Legal Books are a legal library of forms and documents for everyday business and personal needs. E-Z Legal Software provides those same forms on disk for customized documents at the touch of the keyboard.

You can add to your legal savvy and your ability to protect yourself, your loved ones, your business and your property with a range of self-help legal titles available through E-Z Legal Forms. See the product descriptions and order form at the back of this guide.

(***How To Save On Attorney Fees*** **was compiled and written by Valerie Hope Goldstein.**)

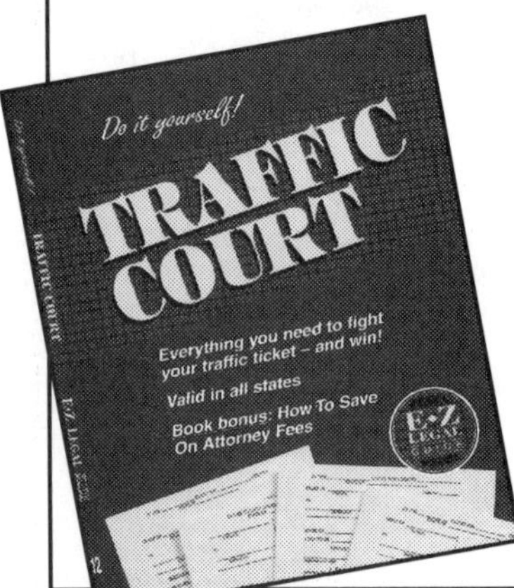

Bankruptcy

How does someone file bankruptcy without adding to their debts? With the *E-Z Legal Guide to Bankruptcy*. Takes the confusion out of bankruptcy by taking the reader through the forms, the law, even the state and federal exemptions.

Stock No.: G100
$14.95 8.5" x 11"
128 pages Soft cover
ISBN 1-56382-400-0

Small Claims Court

The reader prepares for his day in court with this guide, which explains the process for the plaintiff and the defendant, offers options to an actual court case, and more. For anyone who has ever thought about taking someone to court.

Stock No.: G109
$14.95 8.5" x 11"
128 pages Soft cover
ISBN 1-56382-409-4

Employment Law

This is a handy reference for anyone with questions about hiring, wages and benefits, privacy, discrimination, injuries, sexual harassment, unions, and unemployment. Written in simple language from the perspectives of both the employer and the employee.

Stock No.: G112
$14.95 8.5" x 11"
112 pages Soft cover
ISBN 1-56382-412-4

Traffic Court

For most American drivers, traffic tickets are an annoying fact of life. But sometimes the motorist doesn't deserve the ticket. This guide tells how and why to fight a ticket, and how to handle a police stop, read a traffic ticket, and take it to court and win.

Stock No.: G110
$14.95 8.5" x 11"
112 pages Soft cover
ISBN 1-56382-410-8

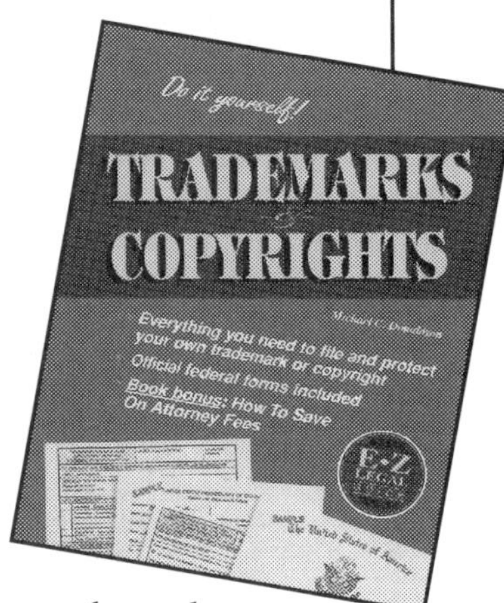

Trademarks and Copyrights

When someone has a great idea and wants to protect it, this book provides the basics of copyright and trademark law: when to get a lawyer, when simply to fill out the right paperwork. Cuts through the volumes of technical information found elsewhere to provide what the layman must know.

Stock No.: G114
$14.95 8.5" x 11"
192 pages Soft cover
ISBN 1-56382-404-3

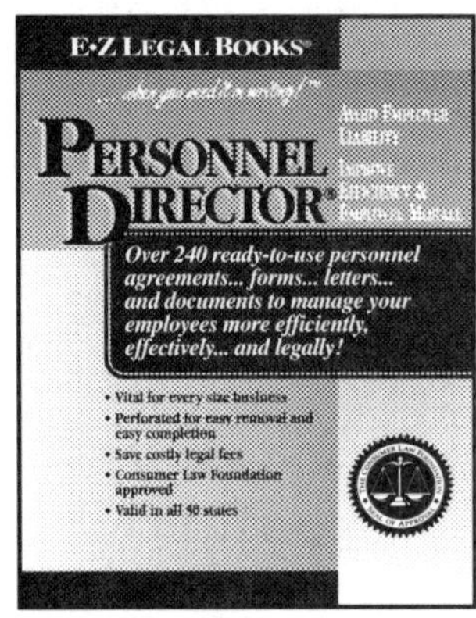

Personnel Director

America's #1 Employee Management System!

Personnel Director manages employees more efficiently, effectively and legally – without expensive legal fees. A collection of over 240 personnel agreements, forms, letters and documents for virtually every size and type of business. Forms document employee turnover, set policy, put agreements in writing and keep all necessary records. Perfect for time-starved small or midsize businesses that want to protect themselves and their employees.

Stock No.: BK302
$24.95 8.5" x 11"
290 pages Soft cover
ISBN 1-56382-302-0

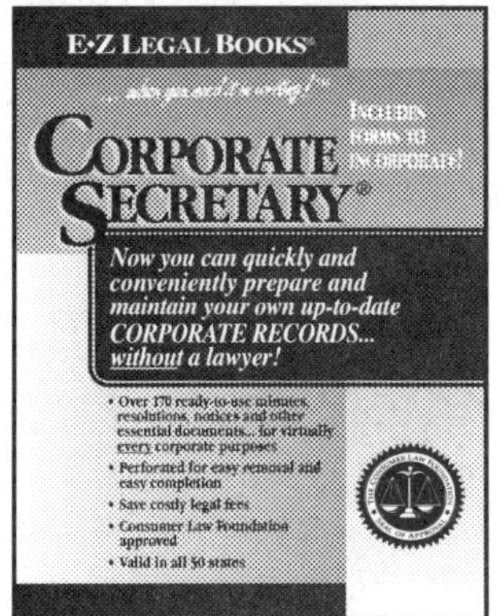

Corporate Secretary

When business owners are ready to incorporate, they don't need a lawyer, they need *Corporate Secretary*. It provides over 170 minutes, resolutions, notices and other essential documents for companies, whether they are small or midsize, private or public, non-profit or for profit, "S" or "C." Helps any corporation hold regular, official meetings and document the votes and transactions of its directors and shareholders.

Stock No.: BK304
$24.95 8.5" x 11"
270 pages Soft cover
ISBN 1-56382-304-7

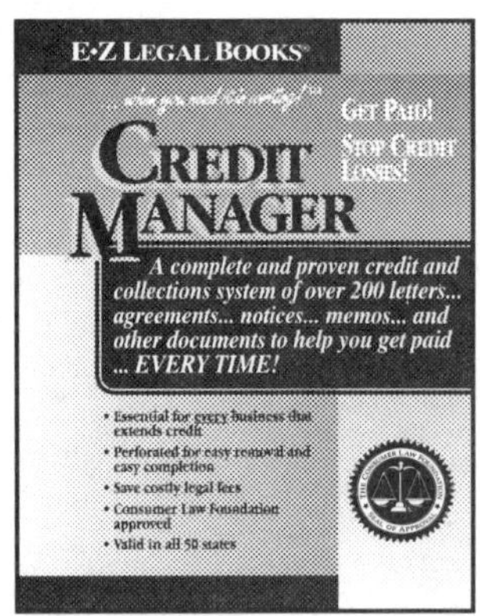

Credit Manager

Business owners stop credit losses and get paid with *Credit Manager*, a complete credit and collection system of over 200 letters, agreements, notices, memos and other documents. *Credit Manager* is for any organization that wants to avoid troublesome disputes and legal liability while enforcing its legal rights and fulfilling legal obligations in credit and collections.

Stock No.: BK303
$24.95 8.5" x 11"
260 pages Soft cover
ISBN 1-56382-303-9

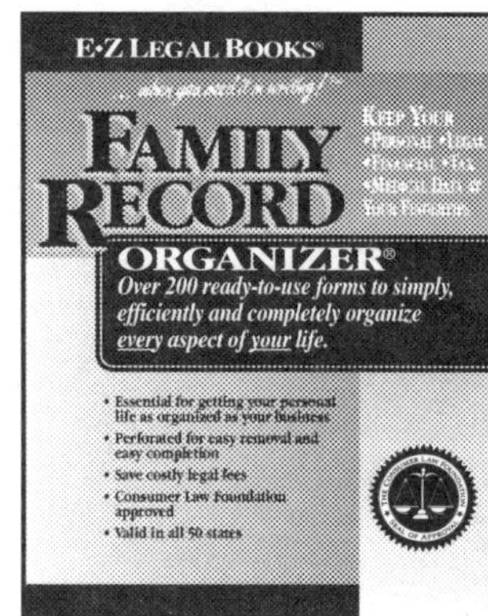

Family Record Organizer

Family Record Organizer contains every form the well-organized household needs to keep life running smoothly, from travel planning to family event scheduling to monthly goal setting. Special sections on business records, investment and financial records, and purchase and maintenance records make it perfect for the home business. E-Z Legal's recordkeeping forms organize every aspect of your life.

Stock No.: BK300
$24.95 8.5" x 11"
226 pages Soft cover
ISBN 1-56382-300-4

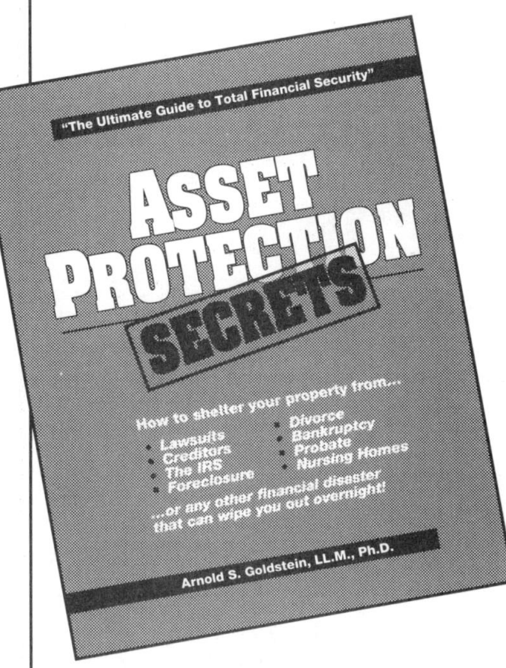

Asset Protection Secrets

This best seller has been featured on over 250 radio and TV shows!

Arnold S. Goldstein, Ph.D.

Asset Protection Secrets reveals all the little-known secrets and perfected strategies guaranteed to protect personal and business assets from financial disaster. This is a full resource guide packed solid with over 230 perfectly legal ways to:

- Become judgment proof.
- Go bankrupt and keep everything!
- Protect assets from IRS seizure.
- Avoid a lawsuit in today's lawsuit-crazy society.
- Leave assets to children so they're fully protected from creditors.
- Shelter property from the IRS, divorce, probate, and creditors.
- Safeguard a business from creditors.
- Shelter wages from attachment.
- Use offshore havens for ironclad financial secrecy and protection.

*D*r. Arnold S. Goldstein is among a select group of distinguished experts recognized for his knowledge of tax and financial protection strategies. Featured on over 400 radio and television shows nationwide, he has authored more than 72 books on law, business and finance.

Founder and President of Wealth$avers, an international financial planning and asset protection organization, Dr. Goldstein also conducts Asset Protection Secrets Seminars nationwide. He is Professor Emeritus at Northeastern University, and teaches asset protection strategies at several colleges and universities. He holds the degrees of Bachelor of Science, Master of Business Administration, Doctor of Jurisprudence, Master of Laws and Ph.D. in law and public policy. He is a member of the Massachusetts and federal bars as well as many professional, academic and civic organizations.

"Asset Protection Secrets is a complete encyclopedia of techniques and tactics to safeguard your assets under all circumstances."
Consumer Law Foundation

"The most important personal finance book this century."
Delray Press

"Asset Protection Secrets is awesome. It really shows people how to build a financial fortress around their wealth."
Robert Itzkow
Taxpayer's Assistance Corp.

Newly revised edition... Updated tax laws and more.

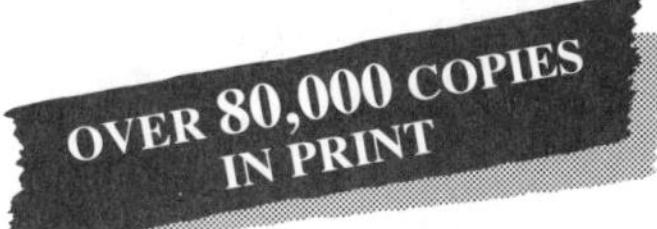

Stock No.: GAPS 100
$29.95 8.5" x 11"
360 pages Soft cover
ISBN 1-880539-004

GARRETT PUBLISHING, INC.

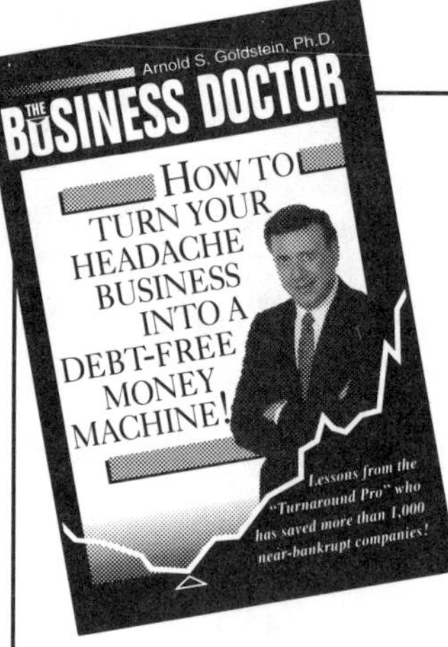

The Business Doctor

Stock No.: TBD 300
$19.95 6" x 9"
326 pages Soft cover
ISBN 1-880539-25-X

The perfect prescription for the ailing business!

Arnold S. Goldstein, Ph.D.

The Business Doctor, loaded with fascinating examples of turnaround successes, is essential for every business owner. From a synopsis of why good companies fail through the step-by-step guide to resolving creditor problems, readers will benefit from its 19 chapters of indispensable, professional advice for owners or managers of financially troubled businesses. Chapters detail how to:

- Sidestep the 10 deadly business killers.
- Turn a business into a creditor-proof fortress.
- Find fast cash for a cash-starved business.
- Avoid Chapter 11.
- Transform losses into huge profits.
- Cash in by selling a troubled business.

...and more!

"Practical advice for those with failing or muddling businesses. This book teaches street fighting skills—your only hope."
Soundview Executive Book Summaries

"Dr. Arnold S. Goldstein has a brilliant reputation in the turnaround field. His strategies should be read by everyone with a faltering business."
Scott Dantuma, President Corporate Financial Recovery, Inc.

Buying and Selling a Business

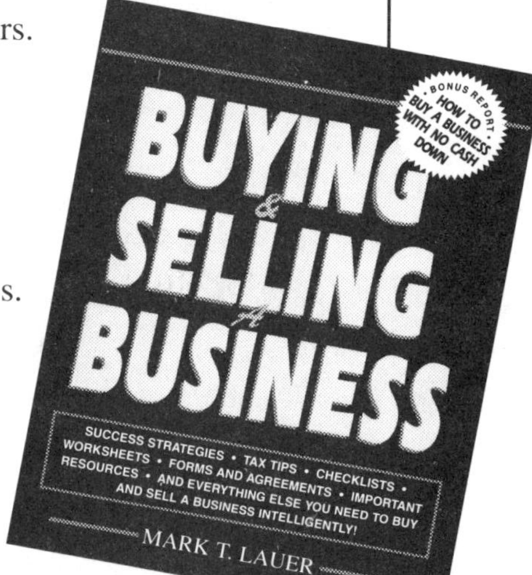

Mark T. Lauer

Clearly written, precisely detailed, with simple guidelines, this book is for anyone considering buying or selling a business. It addresses critical questions such as: "Am I getting the best possible deal?" and "How much will I pay, and when?" The book covers these topics and more as it shows buyers and sellers how to:

- Evaluate and choose the right business.
- Effectively negotiate price and terms.
- Buy a franchised business...intelligently.
- Structure the deal for optimum tax, financial, and legal benefits.
- Find the best financing.
- Avoid the five major pitfalls for business buyers...and the six even bigger pitfalls for sellers.

...and more!

"This book is essential for anyone even thinking about buying or selling a business. It is jam-packed with solid information."
Ken MacKenzie Institute for Business Appraisal

THE BUSINESS BUYER'S/SELLER'S BIBLE

Stock No.: BSB 900
$24.95 8.5" x 11"
256 pages Soft cover
ISBN 1-880539-33-0

GARRETT PUBLISHING, INC.

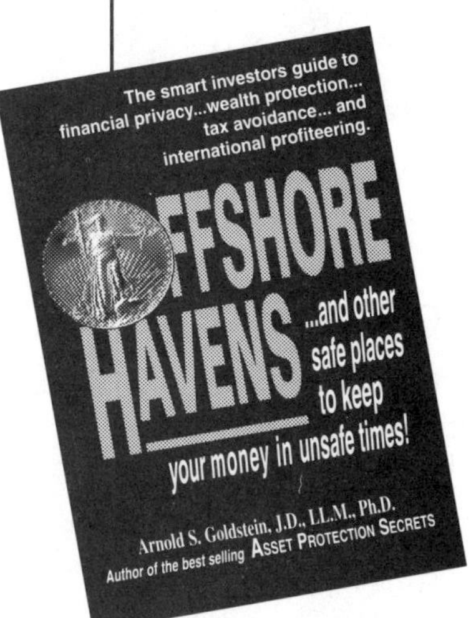

Offshore Havens

A whole new world for wealth protection!

Arnold S. Goldstein, Ph.D.

Offshore Havens helps investors deal with the complexities of offshore financial privacy and international profiteering. As making money within the shores of the United States becomes more cumbersome, foreign investments are expected to grow tremendously. *Offshore Havens* introduces the reader to the dynamic world of international investments and the potential profits found abroad. Among other topics, readers discover:

- The secrets of the ins and outs of foreign money havens.
- Legal ways to avoid taxes and protect assets using offshore havens.
- The best offshore money havens, and why they're so good.
- How to gain privacy and avoid the pitfalls of offshore banking.
- The benefits of conducting your business offshore.
          ...and much more!

Stock No.: OH 700
$29.95 6" x 9"
256 pages Hard cover
ISBN 1-880539-27-6

Includes the latest tax code updates!

Cash for Your Business

Garrett Adams

Written for the small and mid-sized business owner, *Cash for Your Business* reveals the no-holds-barred strategies to win financing from banks, finance companies, venture capitalists, government agencies, partners, and hundreds of little-known sources. The book lists hundreds of financial sources by name, address, and the type of financing offered. It covers new ways to go public with IPD's, SCOR and other programs.

Available at your nearest bookstore, or call 1-800-822-4566.

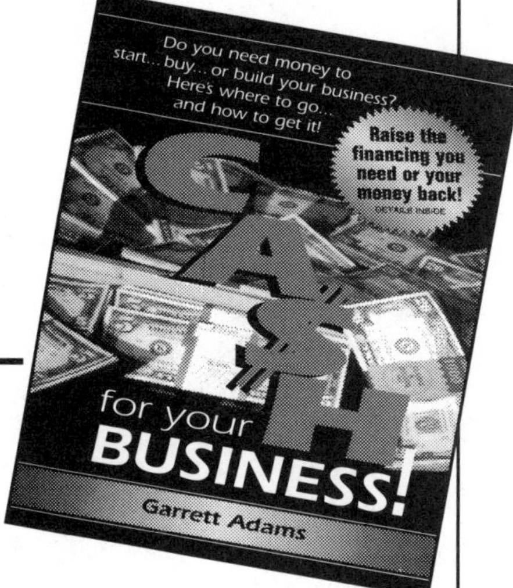

"Cash for Your Business is not just another 'full of theory' finance book. This one precisely delivers the real-world information entrepreneurs need."
Al Cook, Lazarus Corporation

Stock No.: CYB 800
$24.95 8.5" x 11"
256 pages Soft cover
ISBN 1-880539-32-2

 **GARRETT PUBLISHING, INC.**

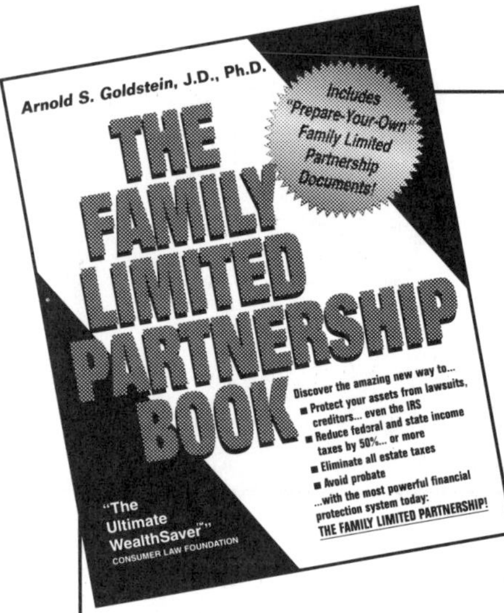

The Family Limited Partnership Book

Stock No.: FLPB 104
$24.95 8.5" x 11"
256 pages Soft cover
ISBN 1-880539-39-X

Lawyers charge up to $6,000 to prepare even a simple family limited partnership. Now it can be prepared in minutes for under $25.

Arnold S. Goldstein, Ph.D.

Family limited partnerships have become the hottest financial planning tool for thousands of Americans. They're the ideal way to protect assets and save income and state taxes while preserving full control of your wealth. Here's the book that teaches how to develop a comprehensive plan to protect your family's assets. Includes easy-to-complete documents to create a family limited partnership, as well as chapters on:

• The benefits of the family limited partnership.
• How to use the family limited partnership for asset protection.
• How to achieve tax savings with the family limited partnership.
• The family limited partnership as an estate planning tool.

...and more!

"Family limited partnerships will soon become even more popular than living trusts."
Financial Facts

Pay Zero Estate Taxes!

Milton Corey - America's #1 financial talk show host.

Pay Zero Estate Taxes shows how to set up an entire estate plan using every tax saving option! Without prior financial planning, the federal government will confiscate a huge chunk of your estate, leaving your heirs with less than half your assets. *Pay Zero Estate Taxes* provides guidelines on:

• Using family trusts to reduce estate taxes.
• How to title assets to reduce taxes.
• Gifting and charitable donations.
• How to fund your retirement to save estate taxes.
• Strategies to plan for nursing home and elder care.
• The 10 biggest mistakes people make in estate planning.
• How to plan before the new tax laws.

...and more!

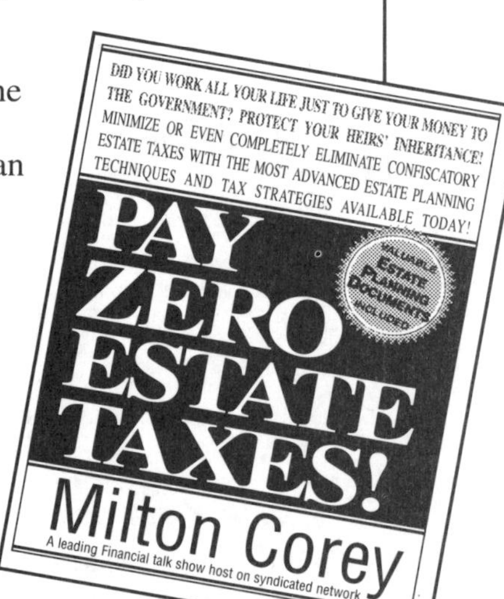

Even middle income families need this book right now. Estate taxes — now 55% on estates over $600,000 — are soon expected to be 70% on estates over $200,000. And this will be retroactive to January 1, 1995!

Stock No.: ZET 800
$24.95 8.5" x 11"
265 pages Soft cover
ISBN 1-880539-28-4

GARRETT PUBLISHING, INC.

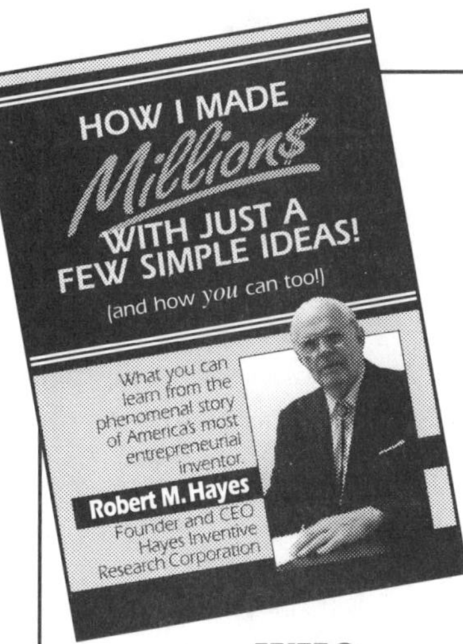

How I Made Millions

with Just a Few Simple Ideas

Turn small ideas into large profits!

Robert M. Hayes

Would-be inventors can take advantage of this well-known author's advice on how to take a simple idea and turn it into MONEY! Covering all phases of modern business, Hayes outlines his hundreds of success stories, and shares inside knowledge that can change failure into triumph.

"The most valuable thing in the world is a good idea...his system shows you how to turn it into MONEY!" **Lloyd MacDonald, Rochester, NY**

"After reading his book, I'm amazed at the wisdom and incredible knowledge covering all phases of modern business." **Beverly Sanders, Ft. Lauderdale, FL**

WHO HASN'T HAD A MILLION-DOLLAR IDEA?

Super Savvy

Maximize employee performance, productivity and profits with this super book.

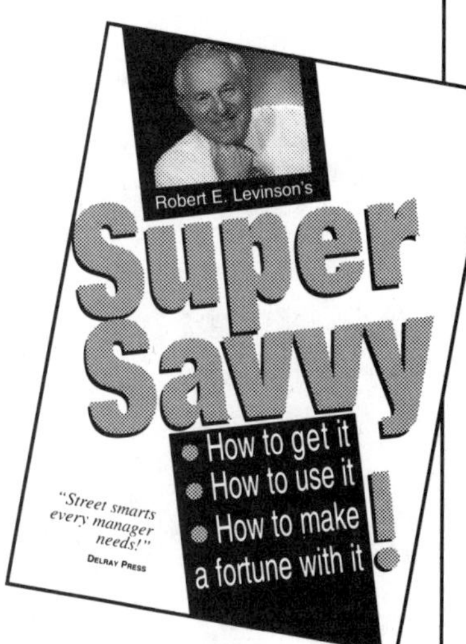

Robert E. Levinson

Levinson's savvy book offers a fresh new approach to "people management" with an insightful perspective on how to get 200 percent from each employee...100 percent of the time. The book teaches modern management principles and emphasizes positive, field tested techniques to get the most out of employees. First-time managers as well as seasoned professionals, can benefit from the principles outlined below:

- Become management savvy and develop team players.
- Be the person everyone comes to for help and advice.
- Spur people to make your goals their goals.
- Spark interest and enthusiasm with job variety.
- Squeeze 70 minutes out of 60.
- Trigger ideas, keep them alive, and translate thoughts into actions.
- Spot the real contributors and develop their potential.

...and more!

"Street smarts every manager needs"
Delray Press

 **GARRETT PUBLISHING, INC.**

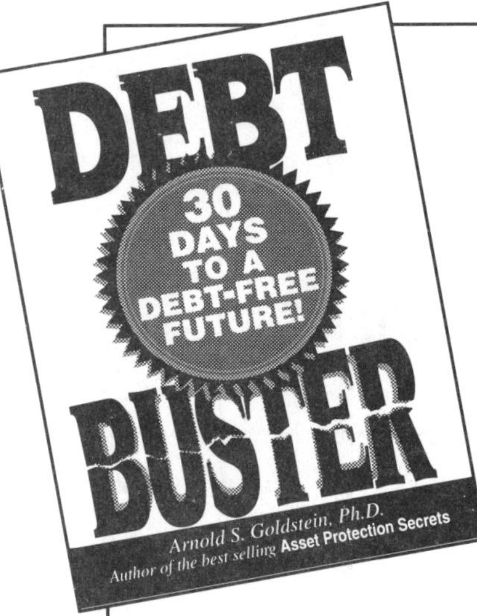

Debt Buster

Stock No.: DBT 600
$24.95   8.5" x 11"
256 pages Soft cover
ISBN 1-880539-26-8

Arnold S. Goldstein, Ph.D.

Debt Buster is a step-by-step guide to getting out of debt without bankruptcy, and managing personal finances efficiently. Here are the solutions for people coping with the daily stress of living from paycheck to paycheck and just making ends meet.

Featured on national television, the Debt Buster program has shown millions of Americans how to:

- Recognize the warning signals of problem debting.
- Protect themselves from bill collectors and negotiate with creditors.
- Use little-known laws to reduce debts.
- Eliminate debt without going broke.
- Avoid bankruptcy, foreclosures, and repossessions.
- Turn credit around, and obtain new credit.
- Protect assets from creditors
                    ...and much more!

Guaranteed Credit

Arnold S. Goldstein, Ph.D.

The perfect book for anyone with less-than-perfect credit. In fact, it's for anyone with no credit history, with any type of credit problem, rejected for credit or charge cards, starting over after bankruptcy, who wants to buy a house or car or apply for a bank loan, whose credit is overextended, or who wants more credit for his or her business!

Guaranteed Credit is a practical step-by-step system to establish, repair, or build credit from America's #1 "money doctor" and the man millions of Americans listen to for financial advice. More than a book on improving credit, *Guaranteed Credit* also explains how to get the best deal when you shop for credit. Finally, the author explains how not to abuse..and lose credit.

*Features a publisher's **money-back guarantee** if credit not improved after 90 days.*

Stock No.: GC 103
$24.95 8.5" x 11"
256 pages Soft cover
ISBN 1-880539-40-3

GARRETT PUBLISHING, INC.

Index

S-W

About the
Author

Valerie Hope Goldstein earned her B.A. degree at Brandeis University in Waltham, Mass., and her graduate degree in public administration from Brandeis' Florence Heller School of Social Welfare. She received paralegal certification from Northeastern University, with specializations in corporate and probate law.

Ms. Goldstein has acted as a legal and financial consultant for numerous organizations. Presently she serves as content analyst for GTE Main Street, one of the first interactive cable systems in the country.

NOTES

NOTES

NOTES

NOTES

NOTES